D1603860

Endorsements

In my experience, governing issues are the number one hindrance to churches being healthy *and* sustaining growth. Tom Lane has been a part of Gateway Church's structure of governance from the beginning, and we have grown and benefited greatly because of his contribution. He has more than 35 years of experience leading churches and is the best person I know to teach others how to have a healthy church government.

ROBERT MORRIS

Founding Senior Pastor

Gateway Church, Dallas/Fort Worth, Texas

Best-selling Author of *The Blessed Life*, *The God I Never Knew*,

Truly Free, and *Frequency*

Have you ever found yourself reading a book on solving a particular problem *after*, not before, you had the problem? Having lived through a devastating church split in which 1,800 of the 3,000 adult members I pastored left the church, taking two million dollars with them and leaving behind incalculable heartache, I wish that I had had a book like the one you hold in your hands. Pastor Tom Lane tackles what might seem to some like a boring subject reserved only for theologians and shows it to be the necessary foundation of any unified, fruitful, and prevailing church. Whether you are an elder, a pastor, or a vital volunteer in your church, and whether your church is large or small—this is a *must read* for all. Grounded firmly in God's Word and proven in real life, coupled with real church examples and practical steps for implementation, this book invites readers to pray for and work toward the most healthy, godly governing of their own churches. At Lifegate Church, it wasn't too late to change. After putting into practice the insights in this book, we have regained and far surpassed the number of people and finances before our split and have experienced the blessings commanded by God (Psalm 133). We have become unified and increasingly mature under the leadership of God's Spirit through a healthy church government. I'm praying for all who read this book to experience the profound blessing it has had on my life and the lives of our leaders and our church.

LES BEAUCHAMP
Senior Pastor, Lifegate Church
Omaha, Nebraska

So much of what I know and practice as a senior pastor and elder at my church, I learned from Tom Lane. He has amazing wisdom and insight into this very vital area of church life. Every pastor, volunteer, and leader need this book.

BRADY BOYD
Senior Pastor, New Life Church
Colorado Springs, Colorado

Pastor Tom Lane is the expert on healthy church government. Having pioneered theocratic government at Trinity Fellowship Church and implemented it at Gateway Church, Tom has run the gamut from startup to a world-impacting mega-church. When I became an elder at Trinity Fellowship in 2002, Pastor Tom was there to show me the ropes. As the current senior pastor of Trinity, I look to Tom as one of the great spiritual fathers of our time. This work is not simply a how-to guide to governance, but it is the culmination of heaven's wisdom, decades of practical experience, and the Heavenly Father's heart expressed through a true sage. This book will help you align your government and strengthen the foundation of your church for generations to come.

JIMMY WITCHER
Senior Pastor, Trinity Fellowship Church
Amarillo, Texas

FOUNDATIONS

OF HEALTHY

CHURCH

GOVERNMENT

With Study Guide

TOM LANE

Foundations of Healthy Church Government
Copyright © 2017 by Tom Lane

ISBN: 978-1-945529-30-6 Paperback
ISBN: 978-1-945529-31-3 eBook
First Edition printed 2017

We hope you hear from the Holy Spirit and receive God's richest blessings from this book by Gateway Press. We want to provide the highest quality resources that take the messages, music, and media of Gateway Church to the world. For more information on other resources from Gateway Publishing, go to gatewaypublishing.com.

Gateway Press, an imprint of Gateway Publishing
700 Blessed Way
Southlake, Texas 76092
gatewaypublishing.com

Dedication

This book is dedicated to Dean Frazier, Elmer Murdoch, and Larry Titus. The legacy of these spiritual fathers has influenced my life and ministry over the years. As significant as the influence of my earthly father and father-in-law in my development has been the influence of these men on my spiritual development and trajectory in ministry. They have watered, planted, and nurtured growth in my life along with others, and I am thankful! To God be the glory!

What then is Apollos? What is Paul? Servants through whom you believed, as the Lord assigned to each. I planted, Apollos watered, but God gave the growth. So neither he who plants nor he who waters is anything, but only God who gives the growth. He who plants and he who waters are one, and each will receive his wages according to his labor. For we are God's fellow workers. You are God's field, God's building (1 Corinthians 3:5–9 ESV).

Table of Contents

Section 4. Building the Organization We Want

Foreword

Jimmy Evans

WHENEVER I INVEST the money and time to purchase and read a book, I want to make sure it is worth it. Most importantly, I want to make sure the author has the authority to speak on the subject. I can attest that this book is a treasure of knowledge and experience from Tom Lane and well worth the investment of your time and resources.

Tom and I have been best friends for the past 38 years. We served together as lay leaders at Trinity Fellowship Church in Amarillo, Texas, for several years before joining the staff together in August 1982. After ten months, I became the senior pastor, and Tom served alongside me as the executive senior pastor for 25 years.

During that time, Tom and I faced the monumental task of moving the church from a dysfunctional, divided, and traditional government model to one that was biblical, functional, and unified. We confronted many challenges in the process, but we faced them together. I am a witness that Tom Lane knows what he is talking about when it comes to church government.

From the beginning, we knew that the process would not be easy, but it was essential. Both of us came to Trinity

Fellowship in the late 1970s, when it was a young, dynamically growing charismatic church. In fact, Tom and his wife, Jan, were one of the original couples who started the church.

Trinity Fellowship was a young and growing church, but it experienced several serious setbacks in those first years because of poor leadership and a faulty church government model. Those issues threatened the church's future and our ability to sustain forward momentum.

That is when Tom and I stepped in to lead the church. As we dealt with the multitude of issues and challenges of a young and growing church, we gave our attention to the task of building a lasting government that God would bless.

One day, in my first few months as senior pastor, I was praying about the church. The Lord spoke these words to me: "Build a model." I must say that the church was such a mess at that point that it was hard for me to think of it as ever being a good model for anyone. Nevertheless, Tom and I led the effort to move things one step at a time toward a biblical, functional, and unified form of government.

Admittedly, we suffered setbacks and experienced surprises. We believed that we could trust some people but discovered that we couldn't. We thought some men were qualified to be elders who weren't. Those discoveries were disappointing, painful, and costly.

In spite of all these things, Tom and I kept encouraging each other not to give up. I can personally say that if I am ever in a fight, I want Tom Lane to be on my side. He is a person of unbending faith, unending loyalty, and unbelievable strength. Day by day and month by month, we worked side by side to build a lasting church government that God would bless.

One day, we woke up and realized it had happened. It wasn't perfect by any means—but it was biblical. It was something we could support through Scripture. It was relational and unified. It was about love and care for one another before it was about decisions, finances, or politics. It was functional—it worked. And it kept working for many years. It provided the foundation for the church to grow dynamically year after year.

Then, in 2000, we planted Robert Morris and Gateway Church in Southlake, Texas. Tom and I had been friends with Robert for many years when he asked if we would plant him in Southlake. Robert stated to us, "I want Gateway Church to have the DNA of Trinity Fellowship in Amarillo." Do you remember what I said about the Lord telling me to build a model?

So, based on the model of government we had built at Trinity Fellowship, we planted Robert and Gateway Church. Tom and I walked every step of the journey with Robert and Gateway Church's elders to plant the church. I can tell you that I've never met a person with more integrity than Robert Morris. He did everything right. He gave detailed attention to dotting the i's and crossing the t's so that the Lord would bless Gateway Church.

And God did! Gateway Church grew dynamically from its first meeting of 40 people in Robert and Debbie's living room. However, after several years of dynamic growth, Gateway Church experienced a leadership crisis. Many wonderful people joined the church, but Robert didn't have the seasoned pastoral leadership and staff to run the church's daily affairs, and it was wearing him out. Then the Lord spoke to Tom and me about Tom going to serve Robert at Gateway Church. So, in 2003, Tom left Trinity Fellowship and moved to Southlake to serve Robert.

Tom immediately brought the maturity and strength Robert needed, and Gateway Church continued to grow dynamically. Even though Robert had totally embraced Trinity Fellowship's governance philosophy, he couldn't do it alone; Tom helped him implement it at Gateway Church as he had done for me at Trinity Fellowship.

Today, both churches continue to grow on the foundation of a stable, biblical government. Tom Lane is a huge part of how it all happened in both places. I give Tom's book my highest recommendation. He is my dear friend, brother, and fellow soldier. I pray it blesses you and helps your church find the government it needs to fulfill its destiny in the Lord.

Acknowledgments

IN MY VOCATIONAL ministry career, I have been blessed to be involved in two great churches—Trinity Fellowship and Gateway Church. Both of these churches have one core foundational element in common: their system of healthy church government.

This book is not just my perspective or an expression of theory. Rather, it is a testimony of over 40 years of relational ministry in the trenches with people who have been mutually committed to God's work through His church. It is my prayer that you are challenged and inspired for your own life, ministry, and church!

As I have written this book, I have reflected on the love and commitment of my wife, Jan. For more than 45 years, she has been my trusted friend and partner, and we have worked hard to lay the same foundational principles in our marriage and family as in the ministries we have served. All of our children love God and are serving Him with their own spouses and children. It is no small thing to note that Trinity Fellowship and Gateway Church were *not* built at the expense of my marriage or children. Instead, they were built on the foundation of a loving, committed (though not perfect) family.

There are many people who have contributed immeasurably to the completion of this project. Thanks to Gateway Publishing, Craig Dunnagan, and particularly John Andersen, who saw the potential for this book as a video resource and championed its development. Thank you to my best friend and colleague in ministry, Jimmy Evans. Thank you to Robert Morris who likewise has been a dear friend, pastor, and colleague. Thank you to the elders of Trinity Fellowship and Gateway Church for the privilege of "doing life" together as we serve God. My greatest joy in ministry has been to serve with my very best friends as spiritual leaders and colleagues. This book is founded on the love and commitment reflected through these men. I am forever blessed by our friendship, and I am eternally grateful for the fruit it has produced!

Introduction

NATIONS, BUSINESSES, CHURCHES, and even families rise and fall because of their governing structures. When institutions are in the incubation stage, it seems as if the governing structure doesn't matter. Everything is organic and pure, with all hands on deck and everybody sacrificing personal interests and perspectives for the good of the whole. Oh, if it could only stay that way! But it can't, and it doesn't. Whether a nation, business, church, or family, a growing institution needs structure to maintain order and processes to guide its decisions. In short, it needs governance.

Gateway Church is one of the fastest growing churches in the United States. It has birthed many new and dynamic ministries for individuals and families. In the middle of all this activity, we have recognized that *church health is more important than numerical growth and church programs.* Church health, coupled with sustained growth, requires governance. At Gateway Church, we recognize that God has a specific plan and purpose for every individual.

Church health is more important than numerical growth and church programs.

Our slogan, "We're All About People," is a recognition that God Himself is all about people. The pressures that come with growth don't change that reality. The apostles recognized this fact in Acts 7 when one group within the dynamically growing Jerusalem church was not receiving proper care. In response, the apostles appointed processes, systems, and structures to meet that need and accommodate the growth.

New levels of growth require systems and processes to care for people and sustain the growth of the church. The broad scope of ministry and the variety of its expressions at Gateway Church simply reflect our desire to care for people. Healthy governance ensures care for people as well as for those who provide the care. We take this approach to ensure the church's impact in our local area and around the world.

God designed the Church to be the hope of the world because it brings His truth for individuals and societies. For a church to have its most powerful impact, it must have a working structure for governing its activities. An individual church will not be able to grow beyond a limited level of attendance or influence if its government won't allow it. Nor can it achieve its full impact of ministry without an effective organizational structure to manage and implement its vision along with the policies and procedures necessary to govern its work.

Nor can it achieve its full impact of ministry without an effective organizational structure to manage and implement its vision along with the policies and procedures necessary to govern its work. Therefore, when a church chooses its government, it molds, shapes, and casts its destiny.

Therefore, when a church chooses its government, it molds, shapes, and casts its destiny.

Church government is the channel from which vision flows for the work of God's kingdom. The church is the collective expression of its members. It carries out its destiny as individuals serve and contribute to God's work through an effective and efficient structure of governance.

Not all church government is equal. What do I mean by the word *healthy* in relation to church government? In this introduction and throughout the subsequent chapters, you will begin to understand the principles of healthy church government. As a foundation for that discussion, it is important to recognize the institutions that God created for our well-being. The church is not an all-inclusive institution, with all authority and control in every aspect of our lives. Instead, it is one of three foundational institutions the Lord established for humanity. He has vested each of these institutions with authority and responsibility in specific areas. Each institution has an important role to play in protecting and sustaining human life. Together, God intends for them to serve as partners working in harmony to fulfill His plan for His creation. These institutions are:

THE FAMILY

God established *the family (the home)* as the first institution. In Genesis, the Lord says:

> "*It is* not good that man should be alone; I will make him a helper comparable to him" (Genesis 2:18).

Later, Jesus explained this passage:

"For this reason [the reason for this relationship] a man shall leave his father and mother and be joined to his wife, and the two shall become one flesh" (Matthew 19:5).

Thus, at the very beginning of the world, God created the institution of the family (the home).

THE GOVERNMENT

God also established *human government.* The apostle Paul writes:

Let everyone be subject to the governing authorities, for there is no authority except that which God has established (Romans 13:1 NIV).

God established governments to maintain human order. He also made them to guide commerce and to add stability, comfort, and protection, thus providing a stable environment for humanity to live.

THE CHURCH

Finally, God established the *Church.* In Matthew's Gospel, Simon Peter declares to Jesus:

"You are the Christ, the Son of the living God" (Matthew 16:16).

Then Jesus replies:

"Blessed are you, Simon Bar-Jonah, for flesh and blood has not revealed *this* to you, but My Father who is in heaven. And I also say to you that you are Peter, and on this rock I will build my Church, and the gates of Hades shall not prevail against it" (Matthew 16:17–18 emphasis added).

Later, Luke notes in Acts:

They continued steadfastly in the apostles' doctrine and fellowship, in the breaking of bread, and in prayers. Then fear came upon every soul, and many wonders and signs were done through the apostles... And the Lord added to the church daily those who were being saved (Acts 2:42–43, 47).

When we consider these three institutions, we can imagine three intersecting circles, each representing one of the institutions.

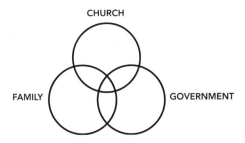

The open areas of each ring represent the autonomous authority of each institution, and the overlapping connected areas identify the interrelationship among them. God ordained each institution to occupy an independent area with authority while simultaneously intersecting in the context of everyday life. Although the focus of this book is the Church, remember that the other two institutions have authority and influence in the human community. Therefore, whenever I address church government or the impact of church leadership on people's lives, I am speaking of a limited sphere of both authority and influence. Although it is a limited sphere, it is an important one that serves as a successful foundation for the other two institutions.

Two Reasons for the Church

What is the unique purpose of the church among these institutions? The church fulfills many important functions, such as making disciples, representing the nature and character of God, and defining and defending the moral landscape of society. However, two primary responsibilities form the foundation for the church to achieve its greatest impact and fruitfulness. If it does not fulfill these two responsibilities, the other institutions will become sterile in their impact on both society and humanity. Therefore, before we discuss the structure and operation of the church, it is critical to acknowledge these two responsibilities.

The Church Is Responsible:

1. To bring the truth of God to bear on the needs of society.

2. To bring purpose and freedom through Christ to individuals who are lost without Him.

The church is the hope of the world. This is not simply a slick statement; I believe it is absolute truth. As the church successfully fulfills these two responsibilities, it also sets the institutions of government and family up for the success God intended. If the church fails, the institutions of government and family will continue to operate, but they will drift aimlessly, having lost the rudder that God intended to hold them to their proper course.

The reality of these responsibilities and their impact is the reason David declares:

> The righteous shall flourish like a palm tree,
> He shall grow like a cedar in Lebanon.
> Those who are planted in the house of the Lord
> Shall flourish in the courts of our God.
> They shall still bear fruit in old age;
> They shall be fresh and flourishing,
> To declare that the Lord is upright;
> *He is* my rock, and *there is* no unrighteousness
>   in Him (Psalm 92:12–15).

Church Government Is Not Optional

God established the church as the foundational institution to further the work of His kingdom on earth. For an individual church to have its most powerful impact, it must have both an organizational structure and systems of thinking that support its ability to govern. A church can only develop its potential as far as its organizational structure and systems of thought will allow. If the church resists the establishment of structure or systems of thought, growth will stop, and dysfunction will inevitably follow.

This dysfunction will cause both new and long-time members to reduce their involvement, ultimately losing their connection with the church. If the church does not have a good understanding of healthy church government or a willingness to change, it will not fulfill its purpose. Committed church members will leave or reduce their involvement because of the vacuum. Even effective ministry programs cannot stop the loss of once-committed members. Ultimately, the dysfunction will constrict a church and compromise its influence.

Church leaders must be willing to embrace organizational change to lead the church to the next level of ministry and to prevent people from slipping out the back door. The potential for members to become discouraged and leave should serve as a motivator for church leaders to form, nurture, and protect a healthy governing structure.

Section 1

A Healthy Church Structure

Chapter One

Three Results
of a Healthy Structure

EVERY CHURCH HAS some form of structure or government, but only a healthy form of government furthers the vision, purpose, and power of God's work in the church. I cannot overemphasize the fact that no church will achieve its optimal ministry effectiveness without a healthy structure of organization and systems of governmental thought that rightly influence and shape the church's operations.

The type of government a church chooses will mold, shape, and cast its destiny. The organizational structure and its governance of the ministry will ultimately determine the work that God can accomplish through that particular church. A church with a healthy organizational structure and system of governance will be able to achieve *three promised important results*:

> *The organizational structure and its governance of the ministry will ultimately determine the work that God can accomplish through that particular church.*

CLEARLY DEFINED AND FULFILLED VISION

A church with a healthy organizational structure and system of governance will be able to *establish a clearly defined vision for itself as well as enable its members to establish vision in their own lives*. Vision for God's work flows out of the church. God designed the church to implement His kingdom's work throughout the earth. Peter writes:

> So I exhort the elders among you, as a fellow elder and a witness of the sufferings of Christ, as well as a partaker in the glory that is going to be revealed: shepherd the flock of God that is among you, exercising oversight, not under compulsion, but willingly, as God would have you; not for shameful gain, but eagerly; not domineering over those in your charge, but being examples to the flock. And when the chief Shepherd appears, you will receive the unfading crown of glory (1 Peter 5:1–4 ESV).

I have heard some people say, "Well, it's not really that big of a deal how I connect to the church, or for that matter, what church I go to, or if I even go to church." As referenced in the introduction, David seemed to have a different opinion. In Psalm 92:12, he says that the people in the house of God will flourish, even in old age.

I want you to make this important connection: God will work out His plans and purposes individually and corporately in connection with the church. I noted earlier that the church does not control everything in your life; however, it does lay the foundation for God's work

4

throughout your life. God will plant you there and cause you to become fruitful and flourish. The church connects you with God's purpose and vision, which will help the other parts of your life make sense.

FORMATION AND DEVELOPMENT OF GOD'S PURPOSE

The church will help you form, develop, and fulfill God's purpose for your life. It will provide a place for service, training, ministry, and connection. The apostle Paul describes an effort made by the believers in Macedonia to give a gift to the church in Jerusalem. He uses their gift as a model to inspire the Corinthian church to join in giving for the benefit of the church in Jerusalem. He writes:

> Moreover, brethren, we make known to you the grace of God bestowed on the churches of Macedonia: that in a great trial of affliction the abundance of their joy and their deep poverty abounded in the riches of their liberality. For I bear witness that according to *their* ability, yes, and beyond *their* ability, *they were* freely willing, imploring us with much urgency that we would receive the gift and the fellowship of the ministering to the saints. And not *only* as we had hoped, but they first gave themselves to the Lord, and *then* to us by the will of God. So, we urged Titus, that as he had begun, so he would also complete this grace in you as well. But as you abound in everything—in faith, in speech, in knowledge, in all diligence, and in your love for us—*see* that you abound in this grace also (2 Corinthians 8:1–7).

The Macedonian church experienced financial and material hardships, yet they gave out of their love for what God was doing, and the church in Jerusalem was the beneficiary. This example of giving helped the Corinthian believers fulfill a part of God's plan for their own congregation. Their giving was inspired, encouraged, and administered by the organizational structure and governmental systems of thought practiced by the church in Macedonia. These wonderful events would never have happened apart from God's governing oversight doing its work in leading, organizing, and instructing the church.

PROVISION OF ORDER AND FOCUS

The church provides order and focus through its structure, which in turn produces effective ministry. The church offers a place for individual believers to find their identity, gives them a platform for ministry service, identifies and develops their gifts, and provides accountability for results. Paul writes:

> "When James, Cephas, and John, who seemed to be pillars, perceived the grace that had been given to me, they gave me and Barnabas the right hand of fellowship, that we *should go* to the Gentiles and they to the circumcised" (Galatians 2:9).

Paul understood the importance of connection and covering for his ministry efforts, so he joined himself to the church. It gave him the platform for his ministry to develop and grow as well as accountability for the ministry results. People often come into the church looking for a covering or some other type of benefit. Through their connection with and work in the church, fruitful ministry develops in their lives. When people connect with the church, positive results happen, or at least the church guides them in the direction that will produce positive results.

Church government provides an underlying structure, which, when properly implemented, leads to fruitful results. No church can realize its full ministry potential without effective organizational structure and systems of thought that allow godly governance. The basis of this structure is the subject of the next chapter.

Three Results
of a Healthy Structure

Key Thought

Every church has some form of structure or government, but only a healthy form of government furthers the vision, purpose, and power of God's work in the church. No church will achieve optimal ministry effectiveness without healthy organizational structure and systems of governmental thought that rightly influence and shape the church's operations.

Summary

This chapter defines three results we can expect when a healthy church structure is in place:
- Clearly defined and fulfilled vision
- Formation and development of God's purpose
- Provision of order and focus

Group Opener

Have the three results of a healthy structure been realized in our church? Are they clearly known and visible?

Group Questions

1. What is the vision statement of our church?
2. How would the average attendee define our church's vision?
3. Are we effectively fulfilling our vision, and if yes, how so?
4. What are the key points that determine if we are fulfilling our vision?
5. How is our church helping people fulfill God's plan and purpose for their lives?
6. What are the effective areas of service, training, ministry, and connection in our church?
7. What are the areas of service, training, ministry, and connection that need improvement?
8. How are we providing order and focus that in turn produce effective ministry?
9. What are some areas that are not producing fruitful results, even though we know they should be present?

Challenge

In the days and weeks ahead, begin to explore on a deep level the questions that have just been asked. God has an incredible plan for your church, but an unhealthy structure can hijack that plan. Continue the dialogue and, together with God's help, realize the solutions.

Prayer

Father, open our hearts and minds to what You are speaking to us about our church. We want Your guidance, Your plan, and Your structure. Give us the grace to discover Your heart for our church. In Jesus' name, Amen.

Chapter Two

Two Foundational Concepts of Healthy Government

Two CONCEPTS ARE vital to the foundation of church government. These principles must be in place to generate and develop support for healthy organizational structure and effective church governance.

Theocratic Rule

The first concept is *theocratic rule*. By this, I simply mean *rule by God*. Theocratic rule acknowledges that God has established all governing institutions as His delegated authorities on earth. Jesus is God, and the Church is Jesus' body, His physical presence through which God works on earth. Accepting and applying the concept of theocratic rule establishes God's rightful authority in our hearts and minds and recognizes His involvement in the operations of the other institutions (family and human government) because He is their Creator.

Other forms of church governance start with humans at the center, as if they, rather than God, had created the institution. A church's form of governance may be presbyterian (rule by a group) or authoritarian (one-person rule); both of these forms are human-centered. However, as in family and government, a church functions best when God is the One in charge:

> Let everyone be subject to the governing authorities, for there is no authority except that which God has established (Romans 13:1 NIV).

God can tell us to *be subject* because He has the rightful authority. He created these institutions; therefore, He has the authority to oversee and direct them. God has the ultimate authority, *and that authority is the essence of theocratic rule.* We can willingly choose to acknowledge His authority as Lord now, or else we will one day be forced to acknowledge His authority as King of kings and Lord of lords. To the Philippian believers, Paul writes:

God has the ultimate authority, and that authority is the essence of theocratic rule.

> Therefore God has highly exalted him and bestowed on him the name that is above every name, so that at the name of Jesus every knee should bow, in heaven and on earth and under the earth, and every tongue confess that Jesus Christ is Lord, to the glory of God the Father (Philippians 2:9–11 ESV).

Theocratic rule is the biblical model of governance and rests on the belief that all leaders are representative authorities of God and His kingdom, rather than of their own kingdoms and selfish interests. As God's representatives, Christian leaders must know that they are subject to His direction and act accordingly. They are His tools for accomplishing His work on earth. The reality is that you can't earn a position as a leader—God appoints, directs, and empowers people for the work of His Church. God leads through a process that we will discuss later, but for now let me say that without a proper process to identify and confirm God's appointment, leaders are merely self-appointed. Self-appointment does not allow us to produce God's work; rather, it opens the door to the enemy's ravaging attacks and resistance. Understanding that all authority in heaven and on earth derives its power from God is the foundation of our spiritual authority. That is why the understanding of theocratic rule is so important—it forms the foundation of healthy church governance. Church governance cannot operate effectively apart from this foundational idea.

Balance of Headship and Team Leadership

The second foundational concept is that of *singular headship*. While we know that team ministry produces results, we also believe that a singular head should guide the team. By singular headship, *we do not mean singular rule*. A unified team of leaders surrounds the singular head to support and assist him.

Embracing singular headship reinforces the understanding that God anoints and appoints one visionary leader to head the institution of a single congregation. Then God surrounds that appointed leader with a team of gifted, committed leaders to aid in the fulfillment of the vision. Paul writes:

> The reason I left you in Crete was that you might put in order what was left unfinished and appoint elders in every town, as I directed you (Titus 1:5 NIV).

At the time of the writing of this letter, Titus was the singular head in Crete, and the appointed elders formed the team around him.

The concept of singular headship finds roots in the Old Testament. God appointed Moses as the leader to deliver His people from Egypt. Biblical scholars estimate that the Hebrews numbered around three million when Moses led them in the Exodus. Imagine the administrative efforts required to move that many people from place to place. Remember, there were no grocery stores, gas stations, or any other conveniences that contemporary people take for granted. Moses' father-in-law, Jethro, confronted Moses for assuming the administrative load as the singular leader. Moses responded to all the Hebrews' needs and settled all their disagreements. Jethro recognized that these responsibilities placed too much of a load on Moses; it was overwhelming him. Jethro served as God's voice, giving Moses the encouragement and support he needed to expand his leadership over so many people:

"The thing that you do *is* not good. Both you and these people who *are* with you will surely wear yourselves out. For this thing *is* too much for you; you are not able to perform it by yourself. Listen now to my voice; I will give you counsel, and God will be with you: Stand before God for the people, so that you may bring the difficulties to God. And you shall teach them the statutes and the laws, and show them the way in which they must walk and the work they must do. Moreover, you shall select from all the people able men, such as fear God, men of truth, hating covetousness; and place *such* over them to be rulers of thousands, rulers of hundreds, rulers of fifties, and rulers of tens. And let them judge the people at all times. Then it will be *that* every great matter they shall bring to you, but every small matter they themselves shall judge. So it will be easier for you, for they will bear *the burden* with you. If you do this thing, and God *so* commands you, then you will be able to endure, and all this people will also go to their place in peace" (Exodus 18:17–23).

This account outlines the concept of a God-appointed singular head who provides visionary and inspiring leadership. But that leader is also surrounded by a group or team of people who undergird and support the work. *Singular headship* refers to a primary person whom God appoints and uses to establish vision, values, and direction for the work.

Sometimes this concept confuses people. They may ask if singular headship means that only one person gets the vision. What about my involvement? Can I have a part in constructing the vision? The answer is yes! The supporting leaders aid in refining the vision that the singular appointed head sets forth. The singular head constructs a skeletal version of the vision. Then, the supporting leaders add flesh, sinew, and all the other components, giving the vision its full body and shaping it as God intended. If construction of the vision falls only to a singular head without the support and influence of a leadership team, then the individual burden is too great and will result in a narrowly-focused vision.

Again, *singular headship* refers to the primary person who establishes the vision, values, and direction for the work. The *plurality of leaders* is a group of leaders who help refine and enact the vision, monitor the priority and timing of its development, and evaluate the results. When the principle of a singular headship with a plurality of leaders is accompanied by *unity*, the church works as God intended. Without unity, the work is reduced to every person doing what seems right in his own eyes. King David writes that it is from the place of unity God commanded His blessing and life forevermore (Psalm 133). When people act with division and disunity, all manner of evil is at work:

> For where jealousy and selfish ambition exist, there will be disorder and every vile practice (James 3:16 ESV).

These are the benefits of *singular headship*:
- Clarity of vision and focus of ministry
- High accountability for the clearly defined vision
- Empowerment for the senior pastor who leads with clearly defined authority

These are the benefits of a *plurality of leaders*:

- High buy-in with shared ownership of the vision
- Input that gives clarity and definition in fleshing out the vision of the leader
- Commitment to the vision from a team of unified leaders and not merely the singular head
- Broad-based support and shared burden for ministry responsibilities

Weakness does not exist *if every person operates within the clearly defined parameters and limits of authority.* Each person must make unity the priority. All governmental systems of thought and organizational structure break down when selfishness and independence drive the process.

Chapter Two Study Guide

Two Foundational Concepts of Healthy Government

Key Thought

Accepting and applying the concept of theocratic rule establishes God's rightful authority in our hearts and minds and recognizes His involvement in the operation of other institutions—family and human government— because He is their Creator. Embracing singular headship reinforces the understanding that God anoints and appoints one visionary leader to head the institution of a single congregation. Then, God surrounds that appointed leader with a team of gifted, committed leaders to aid in the fulfillment of the vision.

Summary

This chapter establishes the first layer of healthy church government. God is at the top and the center, guiding His established leaders who are surrounded by a unified team.

- God is in control, and our guidance and direction ultimately come from Him.
- God establishes His leaders who are His representatives to the Church and the world.
- A plurality of wise counsel surrounding a singular headship brings accountability and shared ownership and vision.

Group Opener

Is God truly at the helm of our church as we follow the lead of a singular headship?

Group Questions

1. How is God involved in the process of governing our church?
2. How is it evident that God has established our church government by His leading?
3. How are we acknowledging God's authority in the way that we govern our church?
4. How can we do better at recognizing God's rule?
5. How are we balancing headship and team leadership at our church?
6. How is our team unified? In what ways is it not?
7. How is our church experiencing clarity of vision and focus of ministry?
8. What shifts might be beneficial to our church government?

Challenge

In the days and weeks ahead, begin to explore on a deep level the questions that have just been considered. God has an incredible plan for your church, but an unhealthy church government can hijack that plan. Continue the dialogue and, together with God's help, realize the solutions.

Prayer

Father, we pray in Jesus' name that You would truly be at the helm of our church. Please guide us as we follow Your lead. Give us the grace to walk in unity behind our leaders. Amen.

Section 2

Identifying the Root

Chapter Three

Extremes of Church Government

THROUGH THIRTY-PLUS YEARS of vocational ministry, I have discovered that most churches form their organizational structure and how they think about governance in response to the previous experiences of a pastor or a founding group. I have observed that they often do not base their church government on biblical concepts; instead, they react to past wounds. When reaction stems from hurt, imbalance results.

Before continuing with descriptions of the extremes of church government, I should say that almost any type of church governance can work if the people have compassionate and loving hearts. My intent is not to suggest that your form of church governance is unworkable for your church's situation. Rather, I want to point out the possibility that it may not have begun with the purest of motives and thought patterns. Recognizing this information is an important step in moving forward.

When leaders carry past hurts and harbor unforgiveness, they find it difficult to keep a pure heart and a clear focus on God's plans. As they consider church governance, they may focus on protection and defense rather than listening to and obeying God. Other forms of governance will work if a leader's heart is compassionate and loving, and God's grace will cover many deficiencies. However, God also wants to help leaders uncover those hidden hurts. As a leader addresses wounds, he may become the catalyst to change his church's structure and revise its system of governance.

> *Other forms of governance will work if a leader's heart is compassionate and loving, and God's grace will cover many deficiencies. However, God also wants to help leaders uncover those hidden hurts.*

When hurts drive leaders' responses, they tend to choose one of two extremes. Either they model the same behavior that caused their wounds, or they become mirror opposites to avoid making similar mistakes and to protect themselves from new wounds. When these extremes are applied to church governance, it is difficult to get healthy input and create a positive church structure. Past pain lives on through this imbalance and typically results in one of the following two types of church government.

Autocracy

Autocracy is church government that concentrates supreme power in the hands of a single individual. *That individual's decisions are not subject to the control of the church's membership or any other leaders.* In a secular society, this form of government would be a dictatorship or absolute monarchy. The only way to remove an autocrat from power is through his own choice, a coup, or his death. An oligarchy is similar, except rule comes from a small group of leaders who are not subject to any other authority.

Autocracy has certain benefits:

- Efficiency in operations and processing of decisions
- Quick decision-making
- If the sole leader has a kind nature and shows benevolence and compassion, it will endear him to the people.

However, autocracy also has these weaknesses:

- Insufficient accountability
- Lack of input from other people who have important expertise
- Little buy-in and ownership from the broader base of leadership and church membership
- A protectionist stance against perceived threats
- If the leader does not have a kind nature, he can be cruel, impetuous, and capricious.

Democracy

Democracy is government by the entire group. Generally, it is group rule through majority vote. In some settings, it is rule by consensus in which every member possesses a "veto" vote. In other situations, the church membership elects a group of leaders in a form of representative democracy, also known as presbyterian governance. In a democracy of that sort, the direction of the church depends on majority rule by the members or presbytery.

Democracy offers these benefits:

- High accountability, with every member having equal authority and responsibility
- High level of input and a balance of perspectives, with every member speaking into the decisions of the church
- High level of buy-in and ownership of decisions from members and church leaders

Democracy also has these weaknesses:

- Limitation and minimization of the pastor's authority, resulting in treatment as a "hired hand"
- Feeling of disempowerment for those in ministry positions (susceptible to the same "hired hand" treatment as the pastor)
- Bureaucratic and inefficient decision-making processes with multiple layers of controls
- Power struggles among members vying for influence and control

What Do I Do Now?

If your church governance falls into one of these two extremes, what should you do? First, recognize that the way to respond to God's convicting work in our lives always begins with acknowledging those things that are out of step with His will. This acknowledgment is also called *repentance*. Your church may have chosen its form of governance in response to past wounds or a church split. Those painful events may have occurred many years ago, and you may not have been present, but they are influ-

First, recognize that the way to respond to God's convicting work in our lives always begins with acknowledging those things that are out of step with His will.

encing how you develop your organizational structure and systems of governmental thought. If you are in this situation, I suggest you do all that you can to reflect on the past, acknowledge any errors, and make as much right as possible. If you are the pastor or a leader in your church, I encourage you to go back to the place and time of the reaction that has produced the current thinking and systems of governance. Acknowledge the extreme reaction without attacking or defending the reasons for it, ask for forgiveness, and seek to make things right.

Second, begin the process of reviewing your current governance system. Avoid making quick changes or fixes. God's work always allows for faith to grow and unity to develop. Remember the "10-80-10 principle." According to this concept, 10% of the church's membership will immediately embrace the change with little or no information or time to absorb it. Another 10% will oppose the change for any number of reasons, and no amount of time or information will change their position. They would not accept change even if Jesus appeared in person to make the appeal. The remaining 80% are sincere, good-intentioned people who want to follow God. They simply need time and information. Lead them in a process that allows understanding and faith to grow toward an obedient response.

The third step may occur simultaneously with the second. Lay a biblical foundation for changing the systems of thought surrounding your church's governance. Teach and preach on singular headship with a plurality of leadership. Allow time to discuss the principles and their application to your current system of government with key leaders. Don't rush the process but also don't allow the 10% who will always resist any change to stall or stymie it. In this step, work in ever-growing concentric circles with your leadership. Begin with the core of your most committed leaders. Place them in a highly relational environment where you can communicate these concepts. Give them context for the change and empower them with the information so that they can influence the rest of the church's membership. Help them to understand the principles behind your efforts and work outward from the core leadership through systematic conversations and presentations.

Finally, be patient, gentle, and kind in leading change. Remember that any change can be scary and difficult. Keep in mind that change of this type also involves a spiritual battle. The enemy will resist your efforts to make the church more responsive to God's vision, leadership, and will. So, pray diligently and often. Guide the church's leadership and membership in a spiritual response to God as it relates to His rule and authority in the church. God will be pleased and honored with the process and will guide you through each step.

Extremes of Church Government

Key Thought

When hurts drive the establishment of church government, leaders tend to choose one of two extremes. Either they model the same behavior that caused their wounds, or they become mirror opposites to avoid making similar mistakes and to protect themselves from new wounds. When these extremes are applied to church governance, it is difficult to get healthy input to create positive church structure. Past pain lives on through this imbalance. This typically results in one of two types of unhealthy church government.

Summary

This chapter describes the extremes of church government. Those two extremes are:

- Autocracy: Church government that concentrates supreme power in the hands of a single individual. That individual's decisions are not subject to the control of the church's membership or any other leaders.

- Democracy: Church government by the entire group. Generally, it is group rule through majority vote.

Group Opener

Does our church government look like an autocracy or a democracy? Do we need to re-visit our structure?

Group Questions

1. On what biblical concepts is our church government based?
2. Are we healthy, or are we reacting to previous negative or painful experiences?
3. How are accountability and buy-in built into our church's government?
4. What are the power struggles within our church's leadership and government?
5. How can majority rule hold back God's will for our church?
6. What areas of health in our structure and government are we missing?
7. How can we implement a review of our church's structure?
8. Who can we reach out to for advice and help in reviewing our structure and government?

Challenge

In the days and weeks ahead, begin to explore on a deep level the questions that have just been asked. Reach out to a third party that is experiencing the health you want to achieve. Continue the dialogue and, together with God's help, realize the solutions.

Prayer

Father, we ask You to reveal the areas in our church where there may be extremes of structure and government. Give us the strength to review and find the areas that need improvement. In Jesus' name, Amen.

Chapter Four

Healthy Tension and Balance

MOST SYSTEMS OF church government fall somewhere along the spectrum of the extremes discussed in the previous chapter. Imagine a bell curve set on a continuum. On one end of the curve is an autocratic style of governance, and on the other end is a democratic style. The peak of the bell lies between the *tension* of those two extremes, representing a *balanced and healthy church governmental system.*

GOVERNMENTAL EXTREMES

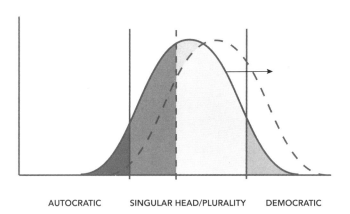

AUTOCRATIC   SINGULAR HEAD/PLURALITY   DEMOCRATIC

Healthy Church Government

Healthy church government exists at the point of balance, or the center point, of the spectrum with equal tension from both ends. The model works together in balance when a plurality of leaders surrounds a singular head. It represents healthy thinking, systems, organizational structure, and processes, which lead the church to respond in full obedience to God's direction.

Once again, I am not attacking either of these other two forms of government. As I said before, any form of government will work if the leaders or members have compassionate hearts and are willing to sacrifice their personal interests. If they do, the character and vision of the church will remain uncompromised, and people will receive love. However, if the model of governance swings to either end of the scale, the work of ministry becomes more difficult to conduct with healthy systems of thought, relationships, and structure. Selflessness is a necessity for hearing, believing, and obeying God. It seldom exists when hurt and unforgiveness lay at a church's foundation. Unresolved wounds can cause the governance to drift or, even worse, to be pushed toward either extreme.

A government with a singular headship and a plurality of leadership creates the right balance and stands apart from autocracy, democracy, and any of their derivatives. Balance is the best

Balance is the best thing that God can give to a church as its foundation for operation.

thing that God can give to a church as its foundation for operation.

Under a single-person rule, efficiency in operation and decision-making may allow the leader to make quick, unilateral decisions. Unfortunately, he can also make decisions too quickly and without the input needed to allow strategic thinking. Such decisions often depend on what the leader may feel on any particular day or what he heard from the last person he met. A pastor who practices single-person rule is empowered because whatever he wants goes—if he needs a raise, he simply tells himself, "I think I need a raise today," and it's done. This system lacks accountability, input from others, and buy-in and ownership of the membership and other leaders.

Group rule by democracy benefits from a high level of accountability—every member has input and buy-in to decisions. However, democracy suffers from slowness of decision-making as it inhibits quick individual decisions in favor of group-ownership. This can lead to leaders who are disincentivized to act creatively because they feel weakness in their leadership, disempowered in decision-making, and treated more like hired help than trusted leaders. Under this form of government, leaders can't move quickly because authorization to act requires buy-in from the majority. The governance process becomes bureaucratic and inefficient, with many layers of control and processes. In addition, this style of government can become highly political with multiple groups vying for influence and control.

Churches with democratic forms of government are usually committee-driven. For example, leaders must submit requests to committees to receive approval before they can implement any new initiatives. For the committee to grant approval, the requestor must then lobby to gain the support of the right members of the committee. The amount of time and difficulty involved in making decisions takes the focus away from hearing, believing, and obeying God.

A balanced approach creates a healthy tension between a singular head and a team of leaders. The singular head establishes the vision, direction, and inspiration for initiatives and assumes leadership within the organization. The plurality of leadership offers stability. One benefit of this approach is a high buy-in with shared ownership of the vision. The singular head still has the responsibility to cast vision and lead the membership toward fulfilling it. However, this system supports high accountability through a clearly defined structure of authority. The structure empowers and protects the senior pastor so that he can lead and make decisions through clearly defined boundaries. The plurality of leadership team is called in to consult or give their input about a decision. Those leaders provide a broad-based perspective, which establishes balance rather than a stifling control process. This tension produces a healthy process of church governance.

At Gateway Church, we describe the levels of leadership and the tension among them in this way: *We are elder governed, senior pastor led, staff and volunteer run, and congregation owned.* We give each of these levels clearly defined roles and responsibilities, and when all groups understand their functions and work together, effective ministry occurs.

The Bible contains several instances of a singular head with a plurality of leadership. As mentioned previously, the Old Testament provides an example of this healthy tension with leaders such as Moses and Jethro. In the New Testament, Peter represents the apostles to the Jerusalem church, and in Revelation, Jesus delivers a letter to the seven churches and references the twenty-four elders. All of these examples illustrate a singular head with a surrounding team of leaders.

Failure to maintain the healthy tension between a singular headship and a team of leaders compromises the church's ability to operate in a balanced way. One side cannot dominate the other; they both must work in harmony. One of the most critical issues facing the health of churches is an ability to understand and keep balanced leadership. Many churches stifle their effectiveness or leave themselves open to destructive forces by operating with a continuous imbalance.

A few years ago, I was speaking with a fellow pastor who had no elders in his church, and he wanted it that way. Without the hindrance of a team to work through, he had no problems accomplishing his own goals. As I mentioned previously, any form of church government will work when the leaders have uncompromised character and are sacrificial in their actions. My friend still has a strong church; it works well, and his people are happy. But there's an inherent weakness. Within his autocratic form of government, my friend has no covering because he's the singular head with absolute, authoritative control. Although he's a nice person, he operates with the attitude, "If you don't like it, get out." As the senior pastor, he is not mean-spirited. In fact, he is very compassionate and caring. He is happy and unencumbered, and his congregation is happy. When members aren't pleased with something taking place in the church, he is cordial and kind but also upfront with his intentions. Everyone knows that "It's his way or the highway."

Even though it is currently functioning satisfactorily, my friend's church has an inherent set of risks. He could leave, die, or do something that disqualifies him as the pastor. Both he and the church have no safety net, covering, or accountability to provide protection. The church might operate without incident for years, but eventually one of the above situations will occur. These disqualifying situations frequently happen in churches dominated by a single leader. And while these events can be somewhat traumatic to any organization, in a church with an unbalanced and unhealthy structure, the results will be devastating.

Where there is no accountability, there is no protection. Nobody is empowered to speak into the pastor's life when problems arise. If something bad happens, it can destroy the good things God has done in that church. At a minimum, it will devastate the people who have put their complete trust in the pastor. With no team to support the pastor, many churches never fully recover, or if they do, it takes years to repair the damage. As the church tries to gather itself after the trauma or tragedy, it will likely react in a protective way to keep something this devastating from ever happening again. Though well-intentioned, these self-protective reactions only add to the destruction. We should trust the pastor as God's appointed person, but that doesn't mean we should accept autocracy and embrace the imbalance that comes from a lack of team support and accountability.

Chapter Four Study Guide

Healthy Tension and Balance

Key Thought

A healthy church government lies in the balanced tension between autocratic and democratic styles of government. Healthy church government exists at the point of balance, or the center point, of the spectrum with equal tension from both ends. This model works when a plurality or team of leaders surrounds a singular head. It represents healthy thinking, systems, organizational structure, and processes, which lead the church to respond in full obedience to God's direction.

Summary

This chapter describes the importance of balance between the two extremes of autocracy and democracy.

- A government with a singular headship and a plurality of leadership creates the right balance and stands apart from autocracy, democracy, and any of their derivatives.
- Balance is the best thing that God can give to a church as its foundation for operation.

Group Opener

Is there a healthy tension and balance in our church government, or do we tend toward one of the extremes?

Group Questions

1. What are the signs (positive or negative) in our church government of an autocratic style?
2. What are the signs (positive or negative) in our church government of a democratic style?
3. Do the positives outweigh the negatives? Explain.
4. How is our church balanced or unbalanced toward one of the extremes?
5. What is the "safety net" in our church if something unexpected happens in the leadership?
6. How can we implement a healthier balance?
7. What are the key areas to focus on for bringing balance?

Challenge

In the days and weeks ahead, begin exploring on a deep level the areas where there is imbalance in your church. Begin a conversation to create buy-in and trust. Discover the answers together as God leads you to the solutions.

Prayer

Father, You are the ultimate source of balance in our ministry and our lives. Lead us on this journey of discovery for the healthy biblical balance that You want in our church government. In Jesus' name, Amen.

Chapter Five

Wounds and Reactions

THE CHURCH IS God's representative on earth. It not only represents God's work, but also it reflects His nature in the conduct of the work. A newly planted church often forms its governmental structure in response to the wounds caused by a previous unhealthy leadership structure. I gave an example of the potential problems of imbalance caused by an autocratic form of government. If the members experienced a dominating leader who controlled, manipulated, and forced his desires on the church, they might be tempted to react by forming a new church and embracing a more presbyterian model. Likewise, if someone was a leader in an unhealthy church, his reaction might be to leave and start a new church under a different structure of governance, with the hope of protection from hurt and devastation. In these situations, both leaders and members leave hurt, frustrated, and even angry, declaring, "We are never going to be part of something like that again."

With that simple inner vow, a leader sets a new course for the future. However, that new course can swing the leader so far to the other end of the church government spectrum as to create a different kind of imbalance. In reaction to a heavy-handed and domineering leader, the new church establishes a democratic form of governance in which each member votes or committees decide everything. The entire church must ratify all decisions. Leaders and members may feel protected in this new form of governance, but this reaction, fueled by hurt and anger from the past, has only led to a new kind of imbalance.

One of my friends led a church with this kind of democratic government. He was afraid to call himself the senior pastor or establish himself as the singular head because of the pain he experienced in a previous church. These unpleasant memories influenced an opposite reaction in which both *everyone and no one was in charge*. That church became a blob, moving indeterminately and without purpose. Because of this dysfunction in its government, the work of the church was stymied. My friend wondered why the church could only grow to a certain level before stalling out. The reason was that no one had the final authority to say, "This is where we are going." Everyone felt that they had equal authority, so every person did what was right in his own eyes, and there was no teamwork or unity of purpose.

Sometimes I will ask, "Why does your church have the government structure that it has?" In response, I hear that the church has based its structure on pain experienced in a previous church. That unhealed wound festers and forms the ideas behind the new church's government, which leaves it vulnerable to problems. The imbalance emerges either as spiritual domination by an individual leader or as a system of political control by a group. The stranglehold created causes a situation whereby God has to work through the gauntlet of political processes and personal agendas. As a rule, God doesn't choose to work through an environment that stifles His purposes. He is King, and we are His servants. The two imbalances of control at either end of the spectrum diminish the church and its government.

A church functions best when it operates in a healthy, balanced tension between a singular head, one who is anointed, blessed, and given godly authority to operate, and a plurality of leaders who give assistance and support to God's work. If a swing to one end or the other of the church government spectrum disrupts this healthy tension, the result is an inevitable breakdown of the systems and structures designed to support the work and growth of the church. The imbalance develops internal mistrust, and the church cannot achieve its vision. When either a dominant head or a political process takes control, it will derail the church from achieving God's purpose.

The rewards of balanced leadership include internal peace, trust, and productivity, which accomplish God's will for that church. A church with a balanced government is a tremendously powerful tool in God's hand. Harmony produces efficiency

> *A church with a balanced government is a tremendously powerful tool in God's hand.*

and enables God's work.

The enemy tries to derail the church by getting the people to choose one of the two polar extremes. Then, he uses that imbalance to spin the church out of control. He happily disrupts the work that God desires to do through that church and its leadership. Balance is one of the church's greatest assets and defenses against the enemy. From that balance, unity grows and produces the blessings of God's presence, favor, and provision for His purposes. When unity and vision exist, God's people can do His work, operate in harmony, and reflect their love for each other. Jesus describes this fruit:

> "By this all will know that you are My disciples, if you have love for one another" (John 13:35).

Think of a tennis net attached to two poles on either side. The way to establish the strength of the net is by turning the crank on the pole, which will adjust the tension at the top of the net and keep it level. Like the taut tennis net, when we establish a balance between singular headship and the plurality of leaders that guide it, the church is kept efficient, focused on God, and impactful of people's lives.

Healthy church government cranks one end of the leadership spectrum to establish the appropriate tension in the governance of the church. It does not happen in a vacuum; it happens in the context of relationships. Balance is achieved and maintained as the tension is tightened through the voice of

Sometimes I will ask, "Why does your church have the government structure that it has?" In response, I hear that the church has based its structure on pain experienced in a previous church.

the singular leader requesting greater authority, which allows a greater ability to function. It takes the slack out of the organizational net, or it may adjust tension by adding greater input through supplying the plurality of leadership more information, enabling them to give timely input on decisions or properly monitor results. Their desire for the information necessary to help them fulfill their function can create tension and even some passionate conversations. It can feel like they are pushing for a more democratic form of governance rather than respecting the role of singular headship to lead and remaining in their function to support and monitor. However, when working properly, relational communication will tighten the tension on the organizational net, thereby maintaining a proper balance between the singular headship and the plurality of leaders.

No church can achieve its best impact, grow to its largest capacity, or develop its full scope of ministry without an organizational structure and system of governance that can support it. The health of its government depends on a godly balance that reflects a tension between singular headship and team leadership. An imbalance brought about by dominance from an individual or a group that rules politically will reduce the effectiveness of the church's operations. There are five necessary elements to achieve this balance of leadership, which I will address in the next five chapters.

Chapter Five Study Guide

Wounds and Reactions

Key Thought

Leaders often react to hurts from a previous church by vowing never to allow the same kind of wounds again. This reaction can cause leaders to start new ventures out of pain rather than the Lord's leading. Reactions often set a course for the opposite extreme, which can be just as unhealthy.

Summary

This chapter explores the ways reactions to past pain can lead to an imbalance in church government. Pain leads to reaction, which then leads to an opposite extreme or imbalance. However, a church with a balanced government is a tremendously powerful tool in God's hand.

Group Opener

How have you responded to wounds that you have received in the church?

Group Questions

1. What conversations or complaints have we heard about the way our church conducts business?
2. What examples of past wounds have we seen that led our church or another church that we know about to choose its style of government?
3. What vows have we heard people make to avoid a past extreme?
4. What positive statements have we heard about our church's form of government?
5. What are some areas where our church likely reacted out of past wounds?
6. What are the key areas to focus on for achieving healthy tension between singular headship and team leadership?

Challenge

In the days and weeks ahead, begin to explore on a deep level the areas where past hurt and pain have caused unhealthy reactions. Begin to seek the honest answers and ask the Lord to guide you toward the truth.

Prayer

Father, we ask You to heal the pain in our church that exists from past unhealthy situations. Give us the grace to expose the pain and create a new balance. In Jesus' name, Amen.

Section 3

Creating Balance

Chapter Six

A Qualified Senior Pastor

WHAT MAKES A qualified senior pastor? Is it his preaching ability? His knowledge of God's Word? His leadership skills? His ability to relate to every generation in the congregation? Yes, to some degree, he must possess all these skills to be effective in leading the church. However, these skills are dependent upon an even more essential foundation that is critical for the senior pastor's success. The skills of the senior pastor must be laid on the foundation of God's call on his life and the process that resulted in him being "sent." Without being both "called" and "sent," he will fall short of the full fruitfulness the Lord intends, regardless of the skills he brings to the position.

> *The skills of the senior pastor must be laid on the foundation of God's call on his life and the process that resulted in him being "sent." Without being both "called" and "sent," he will fall short of the full fruitfulness the Lord intends, regardless of the skills he brings to the position.*

Both Called and Sent

I am always interested in hearing about how God called a pastor into ministry. Clearly, the Lord has a calling for each of us. It is unique and special for each person. Many of the senior pastors I have spoken with have expressed a sense of God's calling to preach. Not preaching feels like disobedience to this call. I have heard some, in an attempt to explain their feelings, quote the apostle Paul:

> I, therefore, the prisoner of the Lord, beseech you to walk worthy of the calling with which you were called (Ephesians 4:1).

These pastors feel that "to walk worthy of the calling" requires them to act. Armed with the belief that God has called them, they move forward to begin their church or step into ministry without being sent. Believing that the call itself is a mandate from God to begin the work, they end up out of God's timing. In the Gospel of John, Jesus speaks 53 times of being sent rather than being called. *The reality is this: a need is not a call. Moreover, a call is not the same as being sent.*

God called the 75-year-old Abraham to be the father of many nations but did not send him until he was 100. Abraham grew anxious and produced a son according to the flesh. The Lord called Moses at age 40 to deliver the children of Israel out of bondage in Egypt but did not send him until he was 80. Moses thought he was personally responsible for the timing of the deliverance, but after taking matters into his own hands at age 40, he had to flee for his life. God called David as a shepherd boy, and Samuel even anointed him as king. However, David served Saul before God sent him to be the king of Israel. The Lord called Joseph in a dream as a teenager but did not send him until age 30.

God calls all of us as servants. He has created every person and given each of us spiritual gifts. God calls each believer to deploy those gifts in service to His people. A *call* relates to *what* God has for us to do, but being *sent* links to *when* God wants us to begin doing His calling for our lives. I have seen many pastors struggling to find God's favor and blessing in their pastoral ministries. When I press them about the process of beginning their ministries, I find that they thought the call and being sent were the same thing. They are not the same. They launched into ministry with a call but were never sent. It is also important to note that you do not send yourself. Another recognized ministry leader should confirm your call, then send you.

A Visionary

A primary responsibility of the senior pastor is to provide visionary leadership to the organization and its members. Among the few things that *only he can do*, this is his number one responsibility. As the singular head of the organization, he receives, communicates, and provides the

> *As the singular head of the organization, he receives, communicates, and provides the visionary direction that enables successful implementation of God's vision by the team that surrounds him.*

visionary direction that enables successful implementation of God's vision by the team that surrounds him. Although a broad base of volunteer and vocational ministry leaders carry out and implement the vision, the senior pastor serves as the primary carrier of the vision to clarify, motivate, and lead people to participate. He communicates and carries the skeletal structure of the vision. It reflects the essential elements necessary to accomplish God's purpose for the church. Then, the larger group of leaders comes together to ratify and further define the expression of his vision. Their input adds the sinew, muscles, and skin. Through this process, the vision is shared and owned by all rather than becoming a driving passion of just one person. God gives the outline of the vision principally to one person and then clarifies, defines, and confirms it through the group.

This process has worked its way out in the establishment and implementation of our vision at Gateway Church in big and small ways, in the larger expression of what we are about, and in the daily work within the organization. The process began when we sat down to define the *master vision*. As the singular head, Pastor Robert Morris expressed the things that God put on his heart through prayer and the Lord's call on his life. As he shared with us, the skeleton of the vision came into view. Pastor Robert articulated the things that God had spoken to him and then had them transcribed into written form. The elders reviewed the document and, through collaboration and conversation, added the ligaments, muscle, and flesh of the vision. For instance, a sentence that began with this simple vision statement about the use of media—"We will impact the world through media"—became this expanded statement:

Gateway Church will reach out through media to serve and equip the Body of Christ and to reach our community and nation with the Gospel. Through television we will address important issues in a way that introduces people to Jesus and His principles for living. We will produce television commercials designed to reach our community for Jesus as well as promote Gateway Church.

Our production services department will grow to excel at all in-house projects, with the goal of producing independent films for broadcast and for theater showings.

We will produce video for the auditorium that makes an impression on the congregation, to educate, inform, and inspire people to get involved in service and ministry for God. We will have live video production capabilities, which will be state of the art.

We will produce videos that make an impression on the congregation as they touch the emotions of people attending. We will produce videos with a message that will have life-changing impact.

We will have the capability of producing videos for every department that support all aspects of ministry, from teaching classes to being able to put an image in front of the imaginations of millions of children that will draw them into relationship with God, and enable them to confidently make right decisions based on biblical values for their lives.

We will be known throughout the world, Christian and secular, for excelling in TV, film, and video, from independent films to music videos to weekly videos that inform with revolutionary style.

Our pastor's simple vision statement about the use of media became, with the collaboration of the elders, the expanded statement of vision, and in the process, the vision became *our vision* (not just Pastor Robert's vision that we support). Pastor Robert provided other statements, and we expounded on those as well.

The vision works its way out in daily leadership interactions as well. When Gateway Church began, the Lord spoke to Pastor Robert and gave him a passage of Scripture as part of the vision for the church. Seven years after he received that Scripture, we were buying property to expand the church's ministry. As we moved forward with negotiations, a sticky situation developed.

We had found a prime piece of property and made an offer to purchase it. Our offer included several conditions along with the purchase price. One of the conditions included the mineral rights associated with the property. We felt we needed them because the mineral rights govern the surface rights of the property. We needed to have control over the surface rights as we created a master plan for the property's development. Therefore, our offer to the landowner included our acquiring the mineral rights. However, when we received the contract, the owners had written it so that they would retain the mineral rights. I pointed the discrepancy out to them and reminded them that our tender offer included acquiring the mineral rights. They asked why we wanted the mineral rights.

I replied that it was because the mineral rights control the surface rights. They rewrote the contract and gave us the mineral rights, but they wanted to retain the royalties. Again, I pointed them to the tender offer that included us keeping both the mineral rights and the royalties. So, they wrote the contract a third time, and this time the contract gave us the mineral rights but split the royalties equally between us. I thought the negotiations might be devolving to a point where if we kept insisting on the conditions of our tender offer, even though they had signed and accepted those conditions, we were going to lose this deal. I called Pastor Robert and updated him on the negotiations. I asked him if it was time to compromise on some of our conditions, and if so, how did he want me to proceed. I needed his input as the visionary leader of our organization.

This is an example of where the senior pastor leads the way in hearing from God for the organization. Pastor Robert replied, "I don't know. Why don't you let me pray about it, and I'll call you back?"

After a couple of hours, he called me and said, "Turn to Deuteronomy 11:14." God had given him this Scripture passage when he started the church. It says, "I will give *you* the rain for your land in its season, the early rain and the latter rain, that you may gather in your grain, your new wine, and your oil." Then Pastor Robert paused and said, "It says 'your oil.' Tom, I've never seen that before. I've read this passage tens, or maybe even hundreds of times, and never seen *oil* in the passage until today. I was asking God to give me the answer to your question, and the Lord said, 'Turn to the passage that I gave you when we started with the church.'" In obedience, he turned to the passage, although he was convinced that he already knew what it said. After we read the passage together, Pastor Robert said to me, "I believe what the Lord is saying is that the oil is ours. So, you can tell the owner of the property that the mineral rights are a deal-breaker. If we don't have the mineral rights and all the royalties, we're going to pass on the deal."

His statement settled in my heart with such peace, and with this direction from the Lord, Pastor Robert both encouraged and empowered me to respond. He told me, "We will not lose this if God wants us to have it. It's God who is speaking to the details of the deal here." So, I called the owner back and told him it was a deal-breaker if we didn't have the mineral rights and all the royalties. The owner's representative replied, "Alright, give me a few minutes, and I'll call you back." About 45 minutes later, he called back and said, "I don't believe it! I have worked for this company for 25 years, and we've never sold a piece of property with the mineral rights and all the royalties. Until now. We're selling this one to you with both the mineral rights and the royalties." Praise the Lord!

Visionary leadership supplies the framework to operate with God's blessing. Coupled with the ability to hear God, it is the first quality a senior pastor needs to lead a church. Everyone must understand that God is the author of the vision. He then speaks it to the person He has called as the singular head and confirms and clarifies it through a group of leaders who have been called to lead with him.

Sometimes people feel that if they cannot speak into the skeletal development of the vision, then they have no real input toward the development of the vision at all. They feel that without the ability to envision the skeleton, they are nothing more than yes-men. That is not the case at all. I am as visionary as I have ever been in my life. I feel that in the process I just described, I have had strategic input into the development of that vision, and, in the end, it is as much my vision as it is Pastor Robert's. My heart bubbles up with excitement and fulfillment as I get to participate in clarifying and confirming the vision God has spoken through our pastor. In reality, although God initiates the vision process through one person, as part of the team, I take ownership of it too. When I talk about the vision, it is not only Pastor Robert's, but it is also mine. *It is ours.* The other elders and I have become a part of the process, which began with God speaking to and through our visionary senior pastor.

Genuinely Submitted

The senior pastor sets the tone for ministry through visionary leadership and clearly defined values for the whole organization. His personal humility and relational accountability set the tone for the whole organization to follow as it implements the vision. When the senior pastor views himself as relationally

When the senior pastor views himself as relationally accountable to the elders and sees them as God's voice to him, then he sets a tone of relational accountability for all the staff to follow in their organizational oversight.

accountable to the elders and sees them as God's voice to him, then he sets a tone of relational accountability for all the staff to follow in their organizational oversight. If he views them as adversarial or as a restraint to God's work, rather than God's voice of confirmation and direction, then a breakdown of authority and, ultimately, progress results. That can flow from him throughout the whole organization. The tension that exists between the singular head and the leadership group that surrounds him is a relational dynamic that requires trust. The elders say, "We trust you. And more than that, we trust God and His work through you in our lives." In turn, the senior pastor says, "I trust you and recognize God's work in my life through you."

When the senior pastor views his position on a matter as God's final statement, there is no room for collaborative input, and others can only support without questioning or resisting his position. As the senior leader, he is praying earnestly over issues; however, no matter how strongly he feels about an issue, he must trust the process. The process will reveal and confirm the timeline for implementation, as well as the scope of the response. Through the process, God will confirm the timing for the decision, or He will reveal additional specifics as discussion takes place and the group of leaders confirms and supports the process.

Genuine submission is a vital character qualification of the senior pastor. He must view the eldership as ultimately responsible to God for the decisions of the church and himself as one voice leading the elders. As the singular leader, it is his role to lead the group of elders to clarity and consensus about God's heart related to the matter through a biblical, timely, and accountable process. This stance enables everyone to view the outcome of the elder discussion and their decision on a matter as God's decision and the confirmation of His will.

Submission is an essential part of the process for everyone involved. Mutual submission between the senior pastor and the elder team around him is what gives the senior pastor confidence to lead. I have observed this dynamic and have been a participant in the process. Our pastor, as the singular head, has the authority to seek God in prayer and deliver with passion and authority what he has heard God say. Once he communicates what he believes, he submits himself to the process and does not feel responsible for pushing his perspective or defending it as God's perspective above any other. He can trust that God will operate through the process to direct those able, capable, and godly men who surround him.

Corporate Leader

Every qualified senior pastor possesses three essential skills:
1. He provides visionary leadership.
2. He spiritually feeds the congregation through preaching and teaching.
3. He relationally connects with people.

Through preaching, teaching, and communicating, the senior pastor must be capable of instructing, inspiring, motivating, and leading both the church membership and its leaders to accept and respond to God's will and the visionary direction He is giving to them. All three skills are necessary for the senior pastor to be fully effective. When our senior pastor speaks to thousands of people, I often hear someone comment that the message was speaking directly to that person! Often that individual will say, "I thought that it was just Pastor Robert and me in the room." This is what I mean when I say that the senior pastor must possess the ability to connect relationally. It is an important qualification for him to lead the membership as well as the organization.

When our senior pastor speaks to thousands of people, I often hear someone comment that the message was speaking directly to that person!

Personal Integrity

Paul writes to Timothy:

> So a church leader must be a man whose life is above reproach. He must be faithful to his wife. He must exercise self-control, live wisely, and have a good reputation. He must enjoy having guests in his home, and he must be able to teach. He must not be a heavy drinker or be violent. He must be gentle, not quarrelsome, and not love money. He must manage his own family well, having children who respect and obey him. For if a man cannot manage his own household,

how can he take care of God's church?
(1 Timothy 3:2–5 NLT).

The senior pastor must demonstrate the character that will enable him to serve as a good example to the members, church staff, and eldership. While perfection is not the standard, integrity is.

At Gateway Church, it is our belief that no matter how greatly a person is gifted, the expression of their gifts can only legitimately rise to the level that the individual's character can support and sustain. The foundation that our gifts and character rest upon is family. Family forms the foundation for ministry and supports the ministry expression that flows from our lives. Both integrity and fruitfulness are necessary for our ministry to be recognized and trusted. These two traits spread over our lives like a roof on a house. If there are holes in the roof or a flawed foundation, then it places the rest of the structure in jeopardy. It will not stand the pressures and storms to come.

We build the structure and expression of ministry upon a foundation of personal integrity, which we reflect in our personal life, marriage, family, attitudes, habits, interpersonal skills, spiritual life, and work ethic. Even more than individual gifting, personal integrity (the character of our lives) is what qualifies us for service to God. Individual and corporate character

> *Even more than individual gifting, personal integrity (the character of our lives) is what qualifies us for service to God.*

must begin with the senior pastor so that it can cascade to every level of the organization. His integrity is the single most important qualification he brings to the ministry— even more than his ability to communicate, lead, or make a relational connection with the congregation.

God called, gifted, and anointed Pastor Robert, but the foundation of his ministry is laid upon the character of his life. In the early years of his vocational ministry, his foundation was flawed, and the Lord knew that it would ultimately put in jeopardy all that He would do through Pastor Robert. This weak foundation was recognized, and he stepped out of vocational ministry for two years to fix it. As his friend for more than 30 years, I know the foundation is now solid. The roof of his life has no leaks, and I am honored to call him my friend and serve on the team that God has assembled to support him.

A Qualified Senior Pastor

Key Thought

God's call and the process of being sent are the foundation upon which the senior pastor exercises his gifts and skills. Without being both called and sent, he will fall short of the full fruitfulness the Lord intends, regardless of the skills he brings to the position.

Summary

This chapter describes the primary ingredients that must be evident in the life and ministry of the senior pastor:

- He must be both called and sent.
- He must be a visionary.
- He must be genuinely submitted.
- He must be a corporate leader.
- He must walk in personal integrity.

Group Opener

If you are not a qualified spiritual elder in your church, the following questions may not apply to you. However, you should read them to see the kinds of issues your pastor and elders are considering.

Group Questions

1. What are some ways we know that God called our senior pastor?
2. What are some ways we know that God sent our senior pastor?
3. As the singular head of the organization, does our senior pastor receive, communicate, and provide the visionary direction that enables successful implementation of God's vision by the team that surrounds him?
4. How do our senior pastor's personal humility and relational accountability set a tone for the whole organization to follow as it implements the vision?
5. How does our senior pastor provide the visionary leadership of spiritually feeding the congregation through preaching, teaching, and relationally connecting with people?
6. Even more than individual gifting, how does our senior pastor's personal integrity (the character of his life) qualify him for service to God?

Challenge

In the days and weeks ahead, begin to explore on a deep level how the senior pastor can grow in all the above areas that must be evident. Be honest and gracious as God leads your team in the personal growth of your pastor.

Prayer

Father, we pray for our senior pastor. We thank You for his life and ask for Your continual blessing on his leadership. We pray for calling, sending, vision, humility, corporate leadership, and personal integrity to be so evident in our pastor's life. In Jesus' name, Amen.

Chapter Seven

Qualified Spiritual Elders

PAUL REMINDS HIS protégé Titus of the work that God has assigned to him:

> This is why I left you in Crete, so that you might put what remained into order, and appoint elders in every town as I directed you. (Titus 1:5 ESV).

The New Testament puts the governance of the church in the hands of elders. These were not simply the older statesmen in the body of believers, nor were they to be the successful businessmen in the body without consideration of their spiritual qualifications. Elders should be the godliest, most committed men in the body of believers, with admirable character and, as their title implies, spiritually mature.

What are the specific qualifications required for the church to appoint someone as an elder? The character of his life should reflect the foundational qualifications listed in two New Testament passages. The apostle Paul writes about them to Titus:

> If anyone is above reproach, the husband of one wife, and his children are believers and not open to the

charge of debauchery or insubordination. For an overseer, as God's steward, must be above reproach. He must not be arrogant or quick-tempered or a drunkard or violent or greedy for gain, but hospitable, a lover of good, self-controlled, upright, holy, and disciplined. He must hold firm to the trustworthy word as taught, so that he may be able to give instruction in sound doctrine and also to rebuke those who contradict it (Titus 1:6–9 ESV).

Paul repeats similar instructions to Timothy:

The saying is trustworthy: If anyone aspires to the office of overseer, he desires a noble task. Therefore an overseer must be above reproach, the husband of one wife, sober-minded, self-controlled, respectable, hospitable, able to teach, not a drunkard, not violent but gentle, not quarrelsome, not a lover of money. He must manage his own household well, with all dignity keeping his children submissive, for if someone does not know how to manage his own household, how will he care for God's church? He must not be a recent convert, or he may become puffed up with conceit and fall into the condemnation of the devil. Moreover, he must be well thought of by outsiders, so that he may not fall into disgrace, into a snare of the devil (1 Timothy 3:1–7 ESV).

Church governance does not equate to managing a business, school, or government agency. The work of the church is at its core a spiritual responsibility, and an obedient response to God's leading and direction fulfills that responsibility. Therefore, to govern the work, it takes spiritual men who are committed to God and reflect His nature and character in their thoughts and actions. A business needs skilled people for its success; a school needs trained educators to achieve its goals; and a government needs administrators with a social perspective. I do not say that these institutions function in a vacuum without the need for character, integrity, faithfulness, and a relationship with God. They are certainly benefitted when godly people are in charge. The church, however, should have the highest standards of godliness for those who lead it. The prophet Isaiah says:

> *Therefore, to govern the work, it takes spiritual men who are committed to God and reflect His nature and character in their thoughts and actions.*

> It shall come to pass in the latter days
> that the mountain of the house of the Lord
> shall be established as the highest of the
>   mountains,
> and shall be lifted up above the hills;
> and all the nations shall flow to it
>   (Isaiah 2:2 ESV).

In their governing role, the elders steward heaven's work on earth. I am thankful that perfection is not required as only One is perfect—the Lord whom we serve. But for the church to fulfill its place as society's exemplary institution, it must have leaders who reflect and demonstrate God's nature through their leadership.

Biblically Qualified and Relationally Centered

Elder governance functions most successfully and powerfully when two important qualities are at the foundation: elders must be biblically qualified and relationally centered. Some churches use criteria that ignore the biblical standards for selecting elders. They give little thought to a candidate's family

> *Elder governance functions most successfully and powerfully when two important qualities are at the foundation: elders must be biblically qualified and relationally centered.*

condition, governing abilities, or financial dealings, let alone his spiritual qualities and character. Instead, choices are based on popularity, standing in the community, or business success.

At Gateway Church, we do not nominate or elect our elders; rather, they are appointed. While it is not wrong to elect them, we appoint them because Paul instructs Titus and Timothy to fulfill the task by appointing elders. Paul does not propose an election. An election poses certain risks. For example, if a group in the church makes a nomination leading up to an election, the process can turn into a popularity contest rather than a selection process focused on identifying the most spiritually qualified candidate. The process may inadvertently imply to those elected that they are responsible to represent those who nominated them rather than God and His work in the church.

Consequently, we follow a process that appoints biblically qualified and relationally connected men who have demonstrated through their service to the church that they recognize spiritual authority over their lives and are committed to the vision of the church. With those qualities evident in an individual, we call them into a place of service.

We use two additional practical criteria for the appointment of elders. First, they must have been actively involved in our church for at least one year. We use this as a guideline, not a law, but feel that it takes about one year to fully understand the vision, work, and call that God has given to Gateway Church. The second quality we use is what we call *chemistry*. We feel that the individuals we add to our elder board should have relational chemistry with the existing group of elders. Chemistry is an intangible mix of relational interaction and dynamics that makes working and being together a joy. It is a measure used by the current group of elders to determine an individual's ability to get along and work with the existing men who make up the elder body.

King David declares that unity is the place from which God commands His blessings:

> Behold, how good and how pleasant *it is*
> For brethren to dwell together in unity!
> *It is* like the precious oil upon the head,
> Running down on the beard,
> The beard of Aaron,
> Running down on the edge of his garments.
> *It is* like the dew of Hermon,
> Descending upon the mountains of Zion;

For there the Lord commanded the blessing—
Life forevermore (Psalm 133).

Unity is such an important principle for how we conduct elder business. We desire every benefit it promises, so we hold on to everything that promotes unity and guard against everything that produces disunity. When we

Unity is such an important principle for how we conduct elder business.

appoint someone, not only must that person have biblical qualifications, but he must also possess a relationally centered attitude with an ability to connect and to get along with and trust the other elders.

One of our operating principles is the belief that relationships are more important than issues. The way this works in the conduct of elder business is this: When discussing an issue, a direction emerges. One elder can say, "You know, I just don't feel good about that direction," and his concern tables or delays the whole process of a decision so that he or the group may gather more information or spend more time in prayer. However, for the sake of unity, we do not allow one individual elder to become a permanent blockage that will keep us from deciding on an issue. Nor are we saying that our definition of unity is *conformity*. Conformity requires each elder to see, think, and process the same, so that every decision looks identical. It provides no place for unique perspectives, creative solutions, or individual giftedness to influence the direction and outcome of a discussion. The Japanese have a proverb that says, "The nail that sticks up gets the hammer." This is the epitome of forced conformity. We encourage an individual to speak up and allow the process to move us all to a place of agreement. Unity does not require conformity; it takes common agreement. We act on common agreement, and this is how unity lives among us.

Where there is biblical unity, there is open debate and diversity of opinion and perspective. The epicenter of lasting unity is a heart for relationships above corporate accomplishment or personal fulfillment. Spiritual unity says:

> I value the relationship I have with you more than I care about producing my result or prevailing over you in our differences. So, if we disagree on this issue, then I want to know why you feel the way you do or see it the way you see it; I want to come to an understanding and then move forward together. I do not want to force a decision before we understand each other. With agreement, we can move forward together.

Additionally, unity does not mean alignment of passion or perspective on an issue. Our feelings on an issue can be strong and yet incomplete. When we come to recognize that perhaps our perspective is not the full perspective, it opens the door to change our opinion. Even though our opinion changes, however, our feelings may lag behind. We become willing to move forward based on the new perspective, even with our emotions still telling us the action is not right. That emotion is based on *stubbornness*. Unity cannot exist alongside stubbornness. Unity exists where there are humility and submission. When we desire unity, and there is an atmosphere of humility and submission, we can ignore our stubborn feelings or, better yet, bring them under the truth we have come to see. We now see differently, through the input of our fellow elders, and a decision can move forward.

One last thought on unity—we must realize that unity does not mean equal passion on all issues. Regardless of the passion we hold toward a decision, we own the decision individually and together. When we hold a decision together, we are unified. When questioned on a decision, we don't recount the process of our discussion. Instead, we simply communicate the decision that was made in unity.

The senior pastor is the *lead elder* among the elders. He is the singular head of every level of leadership in the organization. As the lead elder, he must also hold to unity and apply it to decisions on which he is passionate and convinced that he has heard God. Like the other elders, he must say to himself if he is the one in disagreement, "I trust my fellow elders and God's work through them so much that if I'm the one who's out of step, I will surrender to the mind and the perspective of the elder body." This takes place after the initial discussion and allowing time for further discussion and prayer on the matter. As the chairman of the elders, he will be the one to table the discussion but only after the full expression of opinions and the determination that further time is needed to consider what has been said or to get additional information related to the matter.

Many years ago, while serving on staff at Trinity Fellowship in Amarillo, Texas, I traveled to a conference in

Florida. A matter came up that needed elder attention, and because I was one of the 18 elders, the senior pastor called me and said, "We have a situation that's developed, and I'm calling a special elder meeting. I want to update you on the situation. Please pray and then let me know what you feel." After he explained the circumstances, I said I would call back in the morning and let him know what I was thinking. As I prayed, I felt a clear direction about what needed to take place. So, the next morning when I talked to him, I said, "I prayed, and this is what I feel like God said." Then he said he would represent me at the meeting and share on my behalf how I felt.

When I talked to him the following morning to find out how the meeting went, he said, "Tom, no one agreed with you." I said, "What do you mean no one agreed with me?"

He said, "I mean, I shared what you told me and how you felt, and no one agreed with you." I asked, "No one? Not one person said, 'You know, Tom has a point that maybe we ought to consider.' No one thought I had a good perspective?" He said, "Nope, they understood, but they didn't agree."

Then the pastor asked me what I wanted to do. At that point, I could have insisted on asserting my perspective, believing that I was the one functioning as God's voice. I could have arrogantly said I was the one who is hearing God, allowing myself to think the 17 other men who I know, trust, and conduct life with are deaf on this issue. However, I knew that was not true, and it is arrogance like that which leads to actions that are not under submission and do not reflect unity and its blessings.

Instead, I considered my options. I could have said that I needed more time to pray. I might have said that I'd like to resubmit my perspective for discussion. What I actually said is, "I trust these men, and obviously if 17 men in a unified way are hearing one thing, which is different from what I am hearing, then I must be missing something, and I'll stand down." By "stand down," I meant I would change my perspective to go along with the other men. When I stood down, I owned the decision as if I was one of the 17 who made that decision and not the one who disagreed.

This is how the process of unity works. It is not a matter of saying you're not going to be pressured or bullied into joining or forced to say yes, even though you don't agree. When an elder feels strongly, he must discern what is best—more information, more prayer, yielding his perspective (standing down), or further discussion before moving forward with a decision. There are times when he will need to stand and say, "I just don't have peace. I can't move forward." If he does not have peace and simply cannot move forward, then to stand down and come along with the decision of the other elders would violate his principles. At that point, he must ask for the decision to come to a pause for more information and time to pray. As they pause and pray, God will bring the group into a place of agreement, allowing a unified decision.

We do not put pressure on anyone to move forward as that would violate our commitment to relationships over issues and put unity in jeopardy. We value the unity that we have and the relationships we enjoy more than the issues that we are dealing with or trying to resolve. That deliberation method is the foundation upon which the elder process operates. Simply stated, each elder must align himself with the other members in the process of decision-making. He must trust and commit himself to the other elders with whom God has brought him into relationship. Contention and factiousness have no place in a healthy governance process.

When we appoint an elder at Gateway Church, it is a lifetime appointment, which I will later explain in more detail. The tenure of that appointment is so important to us that it sometimes slows the process of selecting an elder. The need for relational chemistry between the existing elders and an individual under consideration makes the process more tedious than it would be if we elected or appointed elders for a limited term. If elders rotated every three years, we could approach the selection process with a more casual attitude. You might say, "Well, if we get a bad elder, by the time the honeymoon is over, there will only be a year and a half or two years before he's gone." In fact, one friend in a similar situation responded to my question about how his church was going by saying, "I'm two funerals away from revival." He could not wait to rotate a couple of his elders so that harmony, unity, and progress could happen in his church.

Chemistry is an important factor to consider. A person under consideration must fit with the other elders for us to maintain and develop unity. When as an elder, I am dealing with issues that relate to the congregation, ministry, or work that God is doing, I must stand unified with my fellow elders. We imagine ourselves facing each other to find God's will on a matter, but once we have decided, we turn our backs to each other to face the problem or issue. When I envision this, I imagine myself linking my arms with theirs in a circle with each man facing out. If someone wants to attack us, the assault will have to come through someone who knows, loves, and is walking in relationship with me. By facing out in a circle, our backs toward each other, we must fight or defend against someone coming toward us for ourselves and the elders whose backs are facing our own. The way our elder selection process works gives me the confidence to trust in my fellow elders. I am not worried about my back because I know somebody else is guarding it, someone who is committed to me and loves me. That foundation enables us to find the mind of God, walk together in unity, and remain fervent in our love for God and each other.

Non-political

The business of governing the church is spiritual work, not a political process. Therefore, an essential quality for elders is that they have a non-political mindset. An elder must be able to defend the decisions of the group in a rational and fair manner; he must be able to handle disagreements with godliness and character. While conducting the business of the church, if an elder disagrees, he must have the character to express himself honestly and represent his opinions truthfully and lovingly. He should possess these abilities both in leadership meetings and when relating to the rest of the congregation. Paul tells Titus:

> He must hold firm to the trustworthy word as taught, so that he may be able to give instruction in sound

doctrine and also to rebuke those who contradict it (Titus 1:9 ESV).

Suppose I am in an elder meeting, and the group is discussing borrowing some money. As we consider the proposal, the first decision we must make is something like this: "Are we to borrow money as part of God's provision for this need of the ministry?" We must answer the question of whether it is appropriate to borrow money (go into debt) to fund God's work. We must ask each other if we are okay with making that commitment. We must reconcile our personal perspectives on debt with the corporate perspective on debt to move forward on this matter. Then, after fully discussing the issue with openness and honesty, everyone must agree with the decision related to borrowing and the conditions under which it is permissible.

Next, we will ask what amount we are going to borrow. This discussion gets to the root of how much debt we think is reasonable and safe for the ministry. As the discussion unfolds, some may say, "I think we should only borrow this much." And others will say, "Well, I think we can go up to this much." Through the discussion and interaction, we finally come to an agreement. It is the place where we can say, as it does in Scripture, "It seemed good to us and the Holy Spirit" (Acts 15:28). The amount may be a little more than I thought we should borrow, but through the discussion, I have agreed with the amount. I have peace with it. When we take a vote, I represent to the group that I agree with the amount decided, and I own it as if that amount is what I proposed in the first place.

Imagine that I am later with some of the church members. Someone says, "Hey, I heard that we're going to have debt on this project. How does this affect the ministry? I thought you were opposed to debt?" I reply, "Yes, we are. We talked about that as an elder body." Then that person might say, "I heard that it's going to be this amount?" I reply, "Yes, but that is not the amount that I wanted. See, I wanted it to be ..." Suddenly, a crack has developed in the unity of the elder decision process because I have not owned the decision. Instead, I am representing myself and my perspective. If I say, "I know we did that, and it probably wasn't the wisest thing to do. It wasn't what I was thinking, but that's what everybody else decided, so ...," then I have just betrayed my fellow elders in the process. I have stated two things: I agreed with the group, but I was not in unity with them, and I said yes to something in which I did not totally believe.

In other words, I am not on the team. These church members and the spiritual forces arrayed against us now know that if a problem arises, I am not fully committed to the decision the other elders made. Instead, in the face of problems, I could point the finger of blame to make sure that everyone knows it was not my choice so that I don't look bad. The moral of that story is that elders need to own their decisions together and never feel forced to comply with something that they do not agree with as their own. They should make their decisions in an open, honest, and non-political environment that enables each one to own the group's decision.

An elder must not operate secretly or in an unauthorized manner outside of the elder meetings. If an elder attempts to position and posture his perspective among the other elders outside the group meeting, then his efforts are political. Secret maneuvering by a few is divisive and destructive to the foundation of unity. When a person operates outside the open process of shared perspectives among the whole elder body, it is the single most destructive thing that can be done to a healthy governance process founded in singular headship and team leadership.

Political behavior is damaging to the work of the ministry. When an individual elder polls the other elders or goes to members of the congregation to find or build a consensus for a position, especially if he did not build that consensus through open dialogue in the elder meetings, then it is not a pure consensus; it is a political one. If an individual elder is uncomfortable with the direction of a discussion or with a decision that the elders made, then the time to say so is in the meeting. If he does not speak up and ask for a delay for further prayer or more information but instead goes outside the meeting to get verification of his concern and then seeks to build a coalition for his position in order to call for a recall of the decision, then this elder's actions are political and violate the relational commitment to open dialogue and unity within the elder body.

For example, a matter may arise in a meeting, and for whatever reason, an elder does not feel comfortable fully expressing the way he feels. Maybe his justification is, "It bothers me too much to say anything," or "My thoughts weren't solidified enough to express them." And so, he remains quiet about his concern. Then, as soon as the elder meeting is over, he pulls one or two of the elders to the side and says, "You know, when we were talking about that issue, did you agree with that?" The other elder replies, "Well, no, I wasn't comfortable with it, but you know, it's what the pastor wanted, and everyone seemed in agreement with it as we were talking about it." This type of interaction can start a domino effect. Another elder may then join in and ask, "You mean you don't agree with that either?" Suddenly it becomes a political issue; a potential faction has developed, pitting one side against another, simply because the elders in the room were not open and honest as the discussion took place in the meeting. The real meeting is happening outside of the elder meeting through side discussions among some but not all the elders. This is wrong. God works openly, not in secret. His work and will are revealed in the whole truth.

A non-political process simply says *I'm going to speak truthfully. If I receive information outside the meeting that I did not have available at the time of the meeting, I'm going to openly express it to the chairman and ask that we discuss the issue again.* I will not go around and try to convince others to see my side so that I can come back into the elder meeting questioning a previous decision and pushing through a

The moral of that story is that elders need to own their decisions together and never feel forced to comply with something that they do not agree with as their own. They should make their decisions in an open, honest, and non-political environment that enables each one to own the group's decision.

change in the decision, or coming against a decision that the elders already made because now I have the confidence to speak.

An elder assumes the responsibility of governing the work on God's behalf. He is not a representative of a specific group within the congregation. If he takes it upon himself to represent a certain group, he is taking on a political identity as its representative. He makes it his responsibility to represent its needs and wants. Then, he is obligated to report the outcome of his efforts to that group.

Missteps of this kind often begin innocently because of a particular elder's area of interest or involvement. Our elders have wide ranges in their ministry passions, interests, and involvements. One elder may have children in high school who are involved in the youth ministry. Suddenly, innocently and unintentionally, that elder becomes the representative of the youth department as opposed to representing all the ministries in the church. Or maybe an elder is a little older and feels that he is to speak on behalf of people over age 50. It is not wrong for any elder to speak to a concern over a ministry need for a group in the congregation. However, he cannot take it as his responsibility to represent them with bias, for this would limit his ability to govern the whole church's work. A political approach produces a skewed and narrowly focused perspective of ministry. It limits the ability to see the needs of the whole congregation and blocks our ability to see and hear

An elder must remain independent from any group to govern properly.

82

God's voice clearly in the governing process. An elder must remain independent from any group to govern properly. Even if he has an interest and involvement in a specific area, he must care about everybody. Elders govern the whole body and its needs, so they should want to be a part of and understand the needs of all the members. Elders should fairly represent the whole body and all its needs. They cannot become lobbyists in either function or conduct.

Finally, an elder must recognize that his role is to govern, not to monitor mistrustfully. God has called him to come alongside the senior pastor to assist and support him as he leads the church. The senior pastor must recognize that God works through a team, and even as the singular leader, he cannot accomplish all that God wants without a properly functioning team around him. Elders must be careful not to become mistrustful nor to see themselves as God's "watchmen on the wall." Some leaders use that term and believe that God empowers them to watch and suspect the motives of the senior pastor by being watchmen on behalf of the congregation. Some even quote the prophet Isaiah:

> For thus the Lord said to me:
> "Go, set a watchman;
> let him announce what he sees"
> (Isaiah 21:6 ESV).

From this passage, they think that their God-given calling as an elder is to be His "watchman on the wall." This attitude of mistrust will undermine the ability of the elders to walk together in unity. There is no reason to think this passage applies to elders. An elder who carries that attitude is looking at things with suspicion as he questions every motive. We cannot build good relationships on a foundation of mistrust.

Division, dissension, selfishness, and all sorts of other manifestations of evil grow in a negative environment. The apostle Paul says that we should *"put on compassion, kindness, gentleness, humility and patience."* Then he says that we should *"lay aside the unforgiveness and the grievances that we have with one another"* so that we can walk together in unity (Colossians 3:12–13).

While I was praying for our elders one morning during my quiet time, the Lord took me to that passage in Colossians 3. I was praying for unity, covering, direction, and peace. But as I read, the word *grievance* struck me. At that moment, the Holy Spirit said, "You have a grievance that is affecting your ability to walk in relationship with your other elder brothers." I thought, "I'm not offended. I do not wish anybody harm. I am clear. Lord, I'm clear." Then He said, "Look up grievance." So, I did.

A grievance is not necessarily something done to you; it is a perceived injustice that someone may not have even directed toward you, but it is something at which you took offense. Suddenly, the Holy Spirit asked, "Do you remember this situation?" And I replied, "Yes, Lord." Then He said, "You need to lay aside your grievance and forgive your brothers so that you can walk in unity." I went and made that situation right. God promises that compassion, kindness, humility, and gentleness are the qualities of those who walk with clean hearts. We must have clean hearts toward each other if we are going to govern God's work in unity and love.

An elder must be neither controlling nor manipulative in his approach or in the discharge of his governing duties. Each elder must be careful to not take upon himself an attitude of mistrust, nor to see himself as God's "watchman on the wall." Instead, the spirit of an elder must be loving, faith-filled, honest, and committed; these qualities leave no room for mistrust. When an elder cannot trust God's work through the combined voice of the other elders but feels that he must suspiciously protect and watch the work of the ministry or specifically the senior pastor, it is a sign that God has lifted his governmental mantle—or that he never had it.

If we recognize God as the Head of the church, then the singular focus of an elder is to hear, believe, and obey Him. When God speaks, His direction is not controlling nor manipulative; it is gentle, peaceable, and draws us toward His end. When the elders meet, they bring their unique gifts and perspectives to this process of overseeing and governing the church. Through open, honest, and even passionate discussion, their communication allows for the discovery of God's direction as their individual perspectives are shared openly and honestly. In the sharing process, a moment of revelation arrives and produces clarity. Together, the group hears what God is saying. This process enables them to say collectively, "It seemed good to us and the Holy Spirit to take this action."

Called and Anointed

The elder selection process is a spiritual one, undertaken with the same effort that is made in elder meetings to hear, believe, and obey God. God calls men to be elders and anoints them for that work through a selection process. The existing body of elders appoints new ones. The body looks for the spiritual qualities described above,

The elder selection process is a spiritual one, undertaken with the same effort that is made in elder meetings to hear, believe, and obey God.

coupled with relational chemistry and the leading of the Holy Spirit to confirm God's call and anointing on a specific person to join them. They do not select new elders through a nomination process from the membership, as that process makes the selection a popularity contest rather than a spiritual qualification process with the focus on God's choice of an individual.

At Gateway Church, we also appoint elders for life. We do not see a pattern for term-limited service in the New Testament. However, we recognize that elders serve voluntarily, which means that an elder serves until he moves, is disqualified, resigns, or dies. Any of those things indicate that his service is complete and God is moving him to another assignment or place.

Governmentally Gifted

The responsibility to govern is a spiritual gift that comes from God. It is more than simply leadership responsibility, or any leader could do it. It begins with a love for God and His bride, the Church. Spiritual governance requires leadership gifts, which the leader expresses as he gets energy and meaning from governing and overseeing the church. Spiritual leaders understand and respect the authority structure of the church and work within the organizational framework by respecting the role of the senior pastor and the staff he leads. The elder's role is a *governor of the ministry*. Elders should not confuse this with the role of *overseer and implementer of ministry*, which falls to the staff.

In his role as an elder, he must be able to take negative feedback from the church's members and process it without becoming unstable, changing his mind, or becoming ungracious in his responses. He must be able to defend a position without those who oppose it intimidating him or weakening his support of the decision. Elder bodies make many decisions that will affect others and lead them to react. For example, a member may say, "I don't like this," "I do not like the impact of this," "I think we should give greater priority to this," or "I think we should give lesser

> *In his role as an elder, he must be able to take negative feedback from the church's members and process it without becoming unstable, changing his mind, or becoming ungracious in his responses.*

priority to that." When the elder body moves decisively to establish the ministry's direction and priorities, it must communicate graciously and defend those decisions with kindness. They must tactfully say, "I understand what you're saying, but this is what we feel regarding the direction God has given." They cannot let that conversation cause them to waver in their position. Individual elders must have loyal hearts that reflect public support for the senior pastor and the other elders in their interactions with the congregation.

The elders commit to each other and make decisions as a group that reflect an attitude that says *we are all in this together*. They are a band of brothers held together by common responsibilities and love for each other. Elders can even be tempted to think that it is "them" against everybody else. At times like these, they must remind each other that governing does not put them in an adversarial position against the members. However, they also should know that they are not alone in the process. God is with them and loves them. They are partners with a living God who loves and cares for His Church.

Elders walk together in unity, upholding and defending one another, which creates a healthy tension and a stable environment in which the church's government can operate. As they interact with the congregation, they should be honest as they acknowledge the members' feelings or responses. Their feelings may not be right, but the elders should respect them. If their concerns are legitimate, the elders must respond with compassion and openness. An elder should be able to say to members, "I understand what you're saying, and I really do hear your concern." An elder may even say that he has also shared the concern. It is appropriate for him to say, "I understand your concern, and I've also been concerned about that. Yes, we prayerfully considered that issue." These comments do not undermine his ability to defend the elders' decisions. Sometimes the most difficult thing is to say, "I do understand what you're saying." The concerned member may respond, "If you understand what I'm saying, then why didn't you do something other than what you did?" Then an elder must reply by saying something like "Because we believe we heard God and felt Him lead us in a different direction." At times like these, there is nothing more to say. Deep down, the members want the elders to make their decisions as a response to believing, hearing, and obeying God. That is their responsibility, and it is an important part of them being governmentally gifted.

The apostle Peter gives this encouragement:

> The elders who are among you I exhort, I who am a fellow elder and a witness of the sufferings of Christ, and also a partaker of the glory that will be revealed: Shepherd the flock of God which is among you, serving as overseers, not by compulsion but willingly, not for dishonest gain but eagerly; nor as being lords over those entrusted to you, but being examples to the flock; and when the Chief Shepherd appears, you will receive the crown of glory that does not fade away (1 Peter 5:1–4).

Elders have the responsibility to govern the church. They must shepherd the flock of God, otherwise known as the members of the church. This responsibility comes with a reward, but it also includes obligations. They will give an account for how they lead and govern God's flock. He will hold them accountable for the work, and if they govern well, they will receive His reward.

Church Discipline

Earlier in this book, I discussed three major institutions and the authority they have in our lives. God established these institutions and gave them authority to represent Him. Where there is no authority, there can be no accountability. The Church is not the sole authority in an individual's life, but it has some authority given to it by God. It is one of the institutions that He created—the Family, the Government, and *the Church*. The role of the Church is to present the Gospel of the Lord Jesus Christ, make disciples, represent God on earth, and love people on His behalf.

God has given the Church authority to provide spiritual oversight and covering for those individuals who compromise the integrity of the Church in three specific areas:

1. *Those who practice sin as a lifestyle*
   The Church must address and deal with open and blatant sin. The apostle Paul writes:

   It is actually reported that there is sexual immorality among you, and of a kind that is not tolerated even among pagans, for a man has his father's wife. And you are arrogant! Ought you not rather to mourn? Let him who has done this be removed from among you (1 Corinthians 5:1–2 ESV).

Occasionally we receive a call at Gateway Church from someone telling us that one of our members is involved in illegal activities, immoral behavior, or unscrupulous business practices. We do not go searching for this information; we are not God's investigators, nor are we His watchdogs. We do not desire to control people's lives. However, we do have the responsibility to provide spiritual oversight and pastoral input to those who are members of God's church. As elders, we must be good shepherds of the flock of God. In that role, at times, we must lovingly confront members, recognizing them as God's sons and daughters. We ask them to explain their behavior. If we confirm that someone is involved in a sinful lifestyle, our role is to come alongside them and walk with them to a place of freedom and deliverance from that sinful behavior.

2. *Those who deliver false teaching*

The Church must also confront false teaching or doctrinal error (2 Peter 2:1–3). At Gateway Church, we attempt to qualify every person who teaches. We strive to make sure they understand the foundations of Scripture so that they can rightly divide the truth of God's Word. We consider certain theological positions as non-negotiable for those who teach in our church, such as the inerrancy of Scripture and the deity of Christ.

However, we do not require someone to believe and teach everything in the same way. For instance, will the rapture occur pre-, mid-, or post-tribulation? No one actually knows, so we are open to differences. The only thing we would ask is that teachers do not teach personal opinion as dogma, but they should present it as their position and indicate there are other positions as part of balanced teaching. For example, it would be essential for them to believe that Christ will come for His church; however, the time of His return is open for discussion and interpretation.

Some of Gateway Church's members are involved in Bible studies and other learning opportunities that are not a part of the church's program. These meetings may include community Bible studies or home prayer groups. They also involve believers from other churches who are either participants or leaders. If we hear concerns that a group's content or ministry methods are out of step with biblical doctrine, we will take a closer look at each situation.

We may discuss our concerns with an individual who is a member of our church. If we hear multiple reports about the doctrinal content or practices of the group, we will explore the matter further. If we verify the issues that have been brought to our attention, we will speak with any members who are involved and solicit their perspectives. Then, we will clarify our doctrinal position and point out any doctrinal problems we have found with the group.

Upon deeper exploration of the matter, if our conversation confirms that false teaching or questionable practices are part of the group and therefore pose a great danger to our members' spiritual well-being, we will make the members aware of the nature of our concerns.

In all cases, our goal is to provide spiritual care and covering for the church's members, rather than to control their activities and involvement. From a pastoral perspective, if situations like these remain unchecked, they can cause great devastation in the lives of the people whom God has charged us to help, protect, and love. We want to verify the truth of the reports we have heard. So, we engage the members in dialogue and ask, "Do you understand our concern, and are you aware of this error?" We allow time for the members to process our concern, and we work with them to agree about the response to the false teaching or practice and their connection to the group hosting the study.

3. *Those who engage in divisiveness*

The third issue is divisive and contentious behavior within the congregation. Paul says to Titus:

> Reject a factious man after a first and second warning (Titus 3:10 NASB).

Divisive, factious, and contentious behavior is like a cancer in the body of Christ. It may split the church, undermine the leadership, and ultimately hurt every person involved.

I am not referring to someone who exposes illegal, immoral, or unethical behavior within the church and its leadership. If that is the reason for a disagreement, then it is an expression of God's hand of correction. However, we believe that this correction should come through a process involving apostolic intervention, not through the independent efforts of members of the church.

In my experience as a pastor, most factious and divisive behavior stems from a disagreement about the church's direction, involves an effort to build a coalition, and then formulates a strategy to strong-arm the people and the processes to enforce someone's perspective on the church through threats. For example, someone might say:

> "You know, I just don't like the way things are going here, so I am going to gather a group of people to discuss the decisions and direction of the church. If the leadership doesn't change, we are going to withhold our tithe or withdraw our membership."

While I served at Trinity Fellowship in Amarillo, Texas, we had a Christian school as part of the ministry of the church. It had a uniform policy for the students and stated that before students could wear a coat in class, they had to wear an approved uniform sweater. On a cold winter day, one student became chilled but did not have a sweater. The student wanted to wear her coat in the classroom, and the teacher said, "I'm sorry, that doesn't follow the uniform policy. Where's your sweater?" The student replied,

"We didn't buy a sweater. My parents didn't think it was necessary." Then the teacher responded, "Well, you can't wear the coat in the classroom without a sweater. I am sorry, but that is the uniform policy."

The student went home and told her parents about the classroom incident. The teacher's response infuriated the parents, so they decided to assemble a larger group of parents to discuss the matter. The purpose of the group meeting was to threaten the school administration with the withdrawal of their children from the school if it did not fire the teacher and change the policy. Another parent, who was a church member and had a child in the class, heard about the incident and the group of parents. She called the girl's parents and discouraged the group's intended actions, explaining that they did not follow the appropriate process for disagreement and appeal. If continued, the group's behavior would be identified as factious, divisive, and contentious. The school would expel the daughter, and the church would remove the family from membership. This parent explained that the divisive group's actions would not achieve the desired results; she outlined a better way for the girl's parents to express their concern about the school's policies. The influence of this parent put a stop to the group's actions, which could have developed into a very difficult and hurtful situation.

As uncomfortable as these situations are for everyone involved, if elders fail to deal with them, then a sickness develops in the body. Like a rogue cell that mutates and begins attacking healthy cells, factious behavior negatively affects the whole body unless the leaders address it. Left unaddressed, it will metastasize and ultimately have lethal consequences for the body. Do we have differences and disagreements? Absolutely. Are we open to members who approach us to discuss issues of concern? Certainly. However, we do not approach disagreements with a punitive or heavy hand, simply to squelch the problem. Instead, we encourage open dialogue and communication within the proper structures of the organization, which acknowledges a faith-filled dependence on God and respect for the leadership He has put in place.

As our elders provide oversight to families and individuals in the congregation, we take the reports that we hear seriously. If a member is living a lifestyle that God will not bless, we engage them in a way that will provide information, encouragement, and loving care, which will bring about a change in behavior. If a member is attempting to influence others through factious or contentious behavior, we see that behavior as a danger to the congregation that will ultimately undermine the work of the church. In both cases, we need to talk.

Elders have the responsibility to deal with these three matters: sin as a lifestyle, false teaching, and divisiveness in the congregation. Pastoring or shepherding the flock of God in an effective way requires that we address those matters. The apostle Paul says that all members of the church are sinners saved by grace (Romans 3). When I talk about how we address sin at Gateway Church, I often tell people, "We have no sin meters at the doors, and we are not following our members around to evaluate the sin in their lives." However, God is very interested in our behavior. His correction is always motivated by love, and He will begin with us privately as He convicts us and leads us to change. He will work with us to address our sin as an issue just between Him and us. However, if we will not listen, He will broaden the scope of our sin's exposure out of love for us and in response to our procrastination before it becomes harmful to ourselves or the body of Christ. God loves you enough not to let you get away with ongoing sin. He has many ways to make pastoral leaders aware of behavior that they need to address so that they can come alongside believers to help them find freedom and the road to God's blessings in their lives.

Although these are difficult issues, we approach them with gentleness and compassion rather than authoritative heavy-handedness. We have a duty to take action to help the church's members in their relationship with and service to God. Dealing with doctrinal error, factious or conten-

> *Although these are difficult issues, we approach them with gentleness and compassion rather than authoritative heavy-handedness.*

tious behavior, or open sin is part of being a good elder to the flock of God. Being able to confront these issues with mercy, grace, and care is part of being governmentally gifted. When we consider a new elder, if he is unable or unwilling to confront these issues or would confront them in a way that is heavy-handed, we would conclude that he is not governmentally gifted and would remove his name from consideration. Dealing with situations like these is never the fun part of ministry, but we must do it to protect the members of the congregation and fulfill the responsibilities of an elder.

Chapter Seven Study Guide

Qualified Spiritual Elders

Key Thought

The New Testament puts the governance of the church in the hands of elders. These were not simply the older statesmen in the body of believers, nor were they to be the successful businessmen in the body without consideration of their spiritual qualifications. Elders should be the godliest, most committed men in the body of believers, with admirable character and, as their title implies, spiritually mature.

Summary

This chapter discusses the primary ingredients that must be evident in the lives and ministries of qualified spiritual elders:

- They must be both biblically qualified and relationally centered.
- They must be non-political.
- They must be called and anointed.
- They must be governmentally gifted.
- They must provide church discipline.

Group Opener

If you are a qualified spiritual elder in your church, explore the following questions about your elder team.

Group Questions

1. What are some examples of the biblical qualifications of our elders?
2. What are some examples of relational unity among our elders?
3. Are there examples of breakdowns in biblical qualifications or relational unity?
4. Do our elders have a non-political mindset, or are there politics involved? Explain.
5. What are examples of God's calling and anointing on our elders to serve in that capacity?
6. What are some examples of governmental gifting among our elders?
7. What are the ways our elders exercise church discipline with gentleness and compassion rather than authoritative heavy-handedness?

Challenge

In the days and weeks ahead, begin to evaluate on a deep level your elder selection process. Ask God to give you a plan on how to implement healthy change where needed.

Prayer

Father, we pray that You would give us direction as we appoint qualified spiritual elders. Give us the strength to adjust where needed and the wisdom to appoint those whom You have chosen. In Jesus' name, Amen.

Chapter Eight

Elder Engagement with the Organization

THE THIRD ELEMENT for creating a healthy balance is how the elders engage with the organization of the church. Successful administration of the church takes a team. In addition to a qualified senior pastor and qualified elders, a third group ensures success: a gifted ministry team. These are the staff and volunteers who carry out the daily work of the ministry. The elders have a clearly defined role to govern the church, which is separate and distinct from the task of the senior pastor to lead the organization and that of the staff and volunteers to implement the vision through ministry. Each group must know and understand its role to function effectively.

As governors, the elders oversee the ministry results as they manage and prioritize the assets of the church. They function as a group with authority that influences the entire organization. They work through the senior pastor to provide oversight for the staff and volunteers. When the elders meet as a group to oversee church business, they can inquire or give input on any issue related to the church.

They can openly discuss issues, influence the results, ask questions about the methods of ministry, and speak to the effects of any aspect of the ministry on the church's overall vision. Also, they have the authority to pray, teach, and oversee as needed.

However, once they leave an elder meeting, the elders set aside their governmental authority as they relate to the congregation. An elder does not have individual authority in the context of the oversight of church ministries unless he is a pastoral or staff leader of a specific area of ministry. Instead of functioning as an elder, he is a key volunteer working to implement the vision. It is not his role or responsibility as an elder to correct or lead staff members. An elder's general authority within the daily functions of ministry is to lay hands on the sick, pray for wisdom and direction for the members, and teach as needed. He invests and expresses himself in services, such as prayer, altar ministry, and teaching.

Elders must be aware of the esteem they hold with the members of the congregation and staff. They should know that they could intimidate staff members and other volunteers through their service or in the expression of their opinions. Some church members and staff think that if elders express a concern or a perspective during their ministry involvement, they are expressing the position of the elder body with implications for the whole church. However, this is not the case. Elders who engage in ministry serve like any other volunteer under the authority of the pastoral leadership responsible for that area of ministry. They do not have the power to exert governing authority in their daily service in that ministry.

At Gateway Church, we tell staff leaders to put elders to work as trusted lay leaders and to let them use their influence to encourage and impact others. We want to show honor and respect to the elders for their role in the ministry; we want everyone to treat them with the same respect we show all our volunteer members. The organization will not function efficiently if these guidelines are unclear or if individual elders receive preferential treatment over other volunteers. We tell our staff that an elder working with them does not have the authority to move, change, or give ministry direction apart from their direction and approval. That is the authority of their staff ministry oversight.

The senior pastor guides the staff and administration daily. He is the singular head over the staff and the voice of the elder body to them, as well as to the congregation. When we say that we have a singular head, that statement is consistent throughout the organization. At Gateway Church, Robert Morris is the singular head of the elder body, chair of the elders, CEO of our organization, leader of the staff, and senior pastor of the congregation. His singular headship flows in both the direction of the church's oversight and administration of the organization and in the visionary governance of the church through the elder board.

When an elder understands this delineation of duties, he knows that the elder meetings are the appropriate place to express concerns related to the implementation of the vision or the results of ministry. The staff has the responsibility to report information to the elders so that they can effectively monitor and understand the results of the ministry. The elders need this information to evaluate, speak effectively, and act in a timely way. The elders know they should not use their position to direct or correct staff members; that responsibility falls under the senior pastor's leadership and the organizational structure he has put in place.

The senior pastor must have clearly defined parameters and financial authority that enable him to operate effectively in his role as leader of the organization. He must understand where his role of leading the organization ends and his role of leading the board of elders begins. Another benefit of clear parameters is that it gives him protection and accountability as he fulfills his leadership responsibilities.

The senior pastor must have broad limits in his organizational and financial authority. He should have the authority to fill approved staff positions and terminate personnel when needed. His financial authority corresponds to a budgetary process. Each part of the organization submits data at strategic steps in the budget process so that the elders can speak with knowledge into the budget's development. They should have informed approval, as opposed to giving a cursory "rubber stamp" consent to the proposed budget, initiatives, and capital investments.

As the uncontested leader of the church, the senior pastor also functions as a representative of the elder body, implementing the governmental decisions through the organization of the church. He is the mind and the heart of the elder body for the staff and the entire congregation. The senior pastor is the person who connects the elders to the rest of the church.

Elder Engagement with the Organization

Key Thought

The elders have a clearly defined role to govern the church, which is separate and distinct from the task of the senior pastor to lead the organization and that of the staff and volunteers to implement the vision through daily ministry. Each group must know and understand its role for the church to function effectively.

Summary

This chapter discusses the primary function of the elders as a group:

- Elders oversee ministry results.
- Elders manage and prioritize assets.
- Elders work as a group through the senior pastor to provide oversight for the staff and volunteers.
- Elders have group authority, not individual authority apart from the group.

Group Opener

Group authority of elders may be a new concept, or it may require a deeper discussion. Consider the following questions in an open, honest dialogue.

Group Questions

1. How does the concept of group authority challenge the current structure of our eldership?
2. Do our elders exercise authority outside of the group when they individually determine something needs correction? Explain.
3. How do our elders work as a group through our senior pastor?
4. How do our elders operate with care in expressing their individual opinions outside of the group?
5. In what ways is our senior pastor the singular head of the governing elder body, and does he receive their unified respect of that position?
6. How well does our senior pastor understand where his role in leading the organization ends and his role of leading the board of elders begins?
7. What are some clear, healthy adjustments that we can make to our elder structure?

Challenge

In the days and weeks ahead, begin to explore on a deep level how the engagement of the elders with the organization can become healthier. Be willing to have tough conversations, and be open to change.

Prayer

Father, in Jesus' name, we pray that You would give us a clear picture of a healthy elder body for our church. Guide our process and give us the grace to function according to Your direction. Amen.

Chapter Nine

Elder Meetings

THE FOURTH ELEMENT of balance is efficient and effective elder meetings. The senior pastor functions as chair of the elder body. As such, he prepares the meeting agenda and leads the meetings. In his role as chair of the elders, his function is differentiated from his role as senior pastor. As an elder, he has only one vote, the same as the other elders. In his position as chairman, he guides and directs the conversations. He is responsible for leading the group and setting the atmosphere for the meetings, but he is a singular elder with only one vote. He submits himself to the group's unified voice as God's wisdom and confirmation of His direction and will.

Number and Ratio of Elders

At Gateway Church, the number of our elders has varied over the years. Our bylaws state that we will not have less than three elders at any time who also serve as officers of the corporation. When the number of elders exceeds three, then we nominate and elect officers of the corporation from the elder body. The bylaws stipulate no maximum number of elders. The total number of our elders has grown with the church but always with the perspective that the size of the elder body should not become so large that it would impede our ability to walk in relationship with each other and effectively govern the church.

Our bylaws also do not address the mix or ratio of staff to non-staff elders. In the early years of Gateway Church, there was an even balance between staff and non-staff elders. As the church grew, some men from the elder body joined the church's executive team, and it changed the mix toward more staff than non-staff elders. Since we see the role of overseeing the church and its ministries (the staff function) as distinct from governing the work of the ministry (the elder function), the mix of staff to non-staff elders is not a major issue so long as the elders clearly understand their role as different from their role as members of the executive team.

However, non-staff elders do fill one important function in the elder body. They have a more objective perspective that is independent of that of staff members who focus on the day-to-day operations of the ministry. This perspective assists the entire elder body as they evaluate results and monitor financial decisions. At Gateway Church, non-staff elders serve on the compensation committee, which oversees compensation for the senior pastor, executive team, and control parties within the organization.

In the conduct of elder business, any elder may stop the process of an action on any item for further information or additional time to pray. This practice is an important requirement for walking together in unity and applies to financial decisions as much as visionary discussions. It shows that we value relationships more than issues. We will not push an issue through without first considering the relationships we share, which are critical to our unity. We will pause our movement on any item out of respect for the concern or hesitation of any elder. We maintain an attitude of respect for each man's perspective rather than exerting pressure to get a dissenting party to conform to the will of the rest of the elders.

With the separation of duties between governing and managing the daily operations of the church, everyone understands that the elder body does not micromanage the church, nor do they usurp the senior pastor's authority. Elders do not dictate, for instance, what the senior pastor preaches, nor do they determine the staff's schedule or daily responsibilities.

In the everyday management of the church, established policies govern the work. The staff develops the framework for policies, but the elders give final approval.

In the everyday management of the church, established policies govern the work. The staff develops the framework for policies, but the elders give final approval. In this way, they have a voice into the culture of the organization.

Order and Conduct of an Elder Meeting

At Gateway Church, we start our elder meetings by allowing each elder to share personal matters. That sharing leads into a time of worship and culminates in prayer. The priority we give to these practices reflects the *principle of first*, which we believe and teach. This principle means that *we give the first and the best of our lives to God.*

We believe that we should connect with God and each other before we begin the process of governing the church. The church is God's, we are His stewards, and we must never forget that or lose its priority. We also recognize that God blesses a specific model of ministry, which focuses on Him first, makes people the beneficiaries of ministry, and provides resources for the programs, buildings, and assets that we need for the work.

Confidentiality of Business Information

Confidentiality is an essential character quality of every elder. The elders discuss topics and communicate with unguarded openness in the process of their decision-making. We must protect each other's unguarded openness through confidentiality. By confidentiality, I do not mean they have no permission to discuss an item with others. Confidentiality limits sharing to within a limited and defined group. That group includes other elders individually, elders' wives, and the apostolic elders.

Confidentiality is an essential character quality of every elder.

We are free to share the process of our decisions and the details of our discussions with our wives. We are at liberty to discuss and process elder information with our fellow elders. However, we expect each elder to know the ability of his wife to carry the responsibility that comes with confidential information. Information empowers and connects people, which creates the temptation to share confidential information with family or close friends outside the confidential group of members listed above. One could share confidential information as a means of confirming his position of authority or indicating empowerment to a group in the church. However, sharing information with someone who is not part of the problem or the solution constitutes gossip. The enemy uses gossip as a destructive tool to divide people and damage ministry.

Any elder and his spouse may talk to another elder about the processes and decisions of the elder body to help them understand what is happening. They may also talk with Gateway Church's apostolic elders. Elders must recognize their responsibility to handle information properly, knowing that it has the ability either to give life or to destroy people and relationships. Solomon says:

> Death and life are in the power of the tongue,
> and those who love it will eat its fruits
> (Proverbs 18:21 ESV).

The elders are responsible for guarding carefully the way they talk about elder business so that conversations take place in a timely and effective manner that will strengthen, build up, and correct in a life-giving way.

Elder Agenda

The senior pastor, who also chairs the elder body, develops the agenda for elder meetings. The frequency of elder meetings can vary according to the need to address church business in a timely manner. Over the years, Gateway Church elders have met weekly for a couple of hours in the morning before each man went to work. We have also met monthly on a specific day and started in the afternoon, extending late into the night when necessary to address the items on the agenda. Currently, we meet monthly and begin at 11:00 am with worship and prayer. The meeting takes us into a lunch that is provided, and we discuss the agenda while we eat. Most items on the agenda vary from month to month, but a few items recur with regular reports and review by the elders. These regular items include:

- A detailed financial report and analysis
- A campus development report that gives construction updates by campus, along with construction cost discussions and progress reports
- A review of the senior pastor's schedule, which is essentially a report on the ministry expression that he feels the elders should know about and be in agreement with him

Any elder can submit an item for the agenda during the month before the next meeting. He may do it by submitting it to the senior pastor or through a person whom he designates. There is never an attempt by the senior pastor to control the agenda by limiting the ability of an elder to submit an item for discussion. However, consideration is given to the way requests are addressed. Some items are submitted based on a concern for the results of an area of ministry. In such cases, the senior pastor may solicit information from the staff responsible for the area, and he may even ask a staff person from that area to attend the meeting. For this reason, the item may be delayed from the agenda for this process to take place, but the goal is never to hinder someone from expressing the concern or stopping the discussion of the results. It is the responsibility of the senior pastor to determine if items relate to the running of the ministry and implementation of the vision or if they relate to the governance of the church. Those items he determines as related to governance are placed on the elder agenda. Items that relate to the running of the ministry or implementation of the vision are placed on the executive staff agenda for discussion and response. Their response may ultimately make its way into an elder meeting as a written or oral report.

The organization and administration of the elder board must shift and change as the church grows for it to function efficiently and effectively. With a foundation of relational commitment that the elders have for each other, the statement below can be used as a means to identify the need for change:

> If it is working and the elders feel that business is conducted efficiently and on a timely basis, keep doing it; however, if a feeling emerges that the work and the decisions are not made in an efficient and timely manner, then consider the need for change in the time to meet and the length of time to meet.

Values remain consistent, but the methods may need to change for the elder body to be efficient in the governance of the church.

Elder Meetings

Key Thought

Elder meetings are vitally important to the church's continuing function and the implementation of ministry. As chairman of the board, the senior pastor determines the agenda for each meeting and directs the conversation.

Summary

This chapter discusses the importance, structure, and function of the elder meetings:
- Number and ratio of elders
- Order and conduct of an elder meeting
- Confidentiality of business information
- Elder agenda

Group Opener

Like the previous chapter, these questions are designed for discussion by the elders and senior pastor. However, these questions provide important information for every church member. Group authority of the elders may be a new concept, or it may require a deeper discussion. Consider the following questions in an open, honest dialogue.

Group Questions

1. Are the number and ratio of elders working for our church? Why or why not?
2. How does the order of our elder meetings help to create an environment that connects the elders with each other and with God?
3. How well do our elders function in the area of confidentiality?
4. Are the parameters of discussion of confidential information clearly defined? Why or why not?
5. Are there breaches of confidentiality that need to be addressed? If so, what are they?
6. How well does our senior pastor set a clear agenda?
7. How well does the agenda bring top priority matters to the elders' attention?
8. How can we make the meetings more productive with a sense of the presence of God?

Challenge

In the days and weeks ahead, begin to explore on a deep level how your elder meetings are conducted. Begin to make the necessary adjustments. Make it a part of your agenda to explore the structure and function of your meetings.

Prayer

Father, we pray that You would help us see any blind spots in our current elder meeting process. We pray for Your presence as we meet and for complete unity of vision and purpose. In Jesus' name, Amen.

Chapter Ten

Trans-local Accountability

AS A NONDENOMINATIONAL congregation, Gateway Church does not have a connection with an organization that provides a formal structure of oversight and accountability. Without a denominational connection, we have lacked a pool of ministry friends to consult as we lead the ministry. This lack of external structure and relational accountability runs the danger of contradicting something we strongly believe: We believe that God gives as much authority to an individual or group as they submit themselves under. How can we lead with authority apart from a structure that provides relational oversight and accountability? We concluded that we cannot, so we sought a way to establish the oversight and accountability that we were missing by not having a denominational structure.

We believe that God gives as much authority to an individual or group as they submit themselves under.

As we searched the Scriptures, we saw that God works through the ministry of the *apostle* (God's sent one) and the *prophet* (God's agent to build up the church). We determined that the appropriate way to establish external accountability would be through apostolic influence. We began to look for people with whom we already had a connection and who also had trans-local influence in their personal ministries.

We believe that apostolic influence is first and foremost relational. While it has the authority to express itself in oversight, it does not exert itself in a way that controls the local church. Apostolic oversight provides covering and protection through relational oversight in the same way a father gives input to his adult children. A father's oversight and accountability must be founded on respect for his children as adults and with recognition of their ultimate accountability to God.

Even though the local church is autonomous in its responsibility to hear God and determine its ministry vision and direction, it should not stand independent of godly wisdom, input, and relational accountability. It is essential for a church to have an accountable covering to give guidance, wisdom, and a committed, yet unbiased, perspective on ministry initiatives and challenges. If the leadership needs clarity of direction, confirmation of decisions, and objective counsel, then the protection of oversight brings comfort and guarantees safety and health to the ministry. If every church had a covering of this kind, then it would help to protect the pastor and the congregation from imposters who masquerade as friends and supporters but end up hurting and dividing the church. They would have protection from self-inflicted wounds and the enemy's sneak attacks, which try to discredit and destroy God's work through the local church.

The process of selecting one or more people to serve as apostolic elders begins with the senior pastor. The process includes the elders. Both the senior pastor and the elder body must agree on the proposed men, who then become the trans-local oversight to provide accountability when the need arises.

Gateway Church began with three apostolic elders, but after the first few years, two of them transitioned to become local elders of Gateway Church, leaving us with only one apostolic elder. We functioned that way for several years. As the church grew, the team of apostolic elders grew with it. We currently have four apostolic elders who make up our apostolic council. They provide an outside voice for the elder governance of the church. They do not regularly attend our elder meetings, but they have standing invitations to attend any time they desire or if they have something to say to us. On strategic occasions, we invite them to join us and give their thoughts and opinions on a decision so that we will have the benefit of their outside perspective.

We have chosen apostolic elders who are friends of the ministry and have enough familiarity with us to understand matters in the life of our church. We give them the authority to speak into the life and ministry of the church. We do not keep them at arm's length; rather, we invite them into our circle of relationships. For them to know the congregation and develop a corporate relationship with our church, we invite them to speak to the congregation

with some degree of regularity. Through their relationship with the church, they know first-hand the health and
well-being of the leaders of the church as well as the health
and disposition of the congregation.

Our bylaws state that in the normal conduct of elder
business, we make our decisions through majority rule.
However, in practice, we make unanimous consensus
decisions. If we cannot resolve an issue through the
normal relational interactions of the elder body, we have
a process for appealing to our apostolic elders. When we
make such an appeal, we know their decision will serve as
God's voice to us on the matter and will be final. We believe
in the role of the apostolic elder so much that we have
formalized it in our bylaws, as seen in 4.3.1:

> Resolving governing disputes among the elders:
> In any dispute arising among the elders relating to
> the governance of the church and the office of the
> senior pastor, all parties involved will cooperate in
> good faith to resolve the dispute. When an issue is
> determined to be at an impasse, the first appeal is to
> the chairman of our apostolic council of elders. At
> his discretion, the full apostolic council is invited to
> speak into the issue for the purpose of arriving at a
> unified decision. Their decision is final.

It is essential for our overseers to retain the ability
to provide actual accountability, which means that the
apostolic elders must be regularly present and vested with
the authority to speak into the life of the church. When
our elder body arrives at an impasse on a matter, we may

pause the process and, if necessary, ask for help from the apostolic elders. If a matter becomes too emotionally volatile for our elder body to resolve on our own, we can say that maybe we're too close to the issue. At that point, we will pause the discussion, lay down our personal perspectives and pride, and join together in our commitment to hear what God is saying. Our unified desire to hear God leads us to seek counsel and clarity from our apostolic oversight.

The ability to appeal to the apostolic elders in our governing process provides a healthy tension for our accountability that works for Gateway Church. Things may be moving along smoothly when we encounter an issue that we cannot resolve. We need a neutral third party who knows us, loves us, and can guide us around some potential pitfalls. Our apostolic elders serve as a voice of reason, warning, and confirmation for God's work among us. Their oversight provides wisdom and protection for the ministry and is an integral part of our healthy church government.

In addition to accountability, our apostolic elders give covering in times of crisis. No church can foresee every crisis it might experience. A crisis can traumatize the congregation and staff. The crisis could be the death of the senior pastor or the moral failing of a key leader. The crisis could arise from an accusation by a member or an influential leader or an attack on the ministry from an increasingly hostile secular society. Accusations can escalate to the point where lines are drawn and someone takes divisive action. The apostolic elders step in to provide covering, comfort, and stability to the staff, congregation, and outside sources whenever these crises occur. The support of the apostolic elders lets everyone know that we are not alone in our ministry efforts, nor do we act independently.

The apostolic council has both a spiritual and a relational role. Their role is *spiritual* because they give benefit and covering to the work of the local church. They have a *relational* role that is recognized by the senior pastor and affirmed by the elders as part of the process of accountability in governing the work of the church.

The duties of an apostolic elder are:
- To give objective input on major issues affecting the church
- To arbitrate disputes that cannot be internally resolved within the leadership and between the congregation and the leadership
- To give perspective to the significant life issues of the church
- To serve as a support resource and give counsel to the senior pastor as he leads and to the elders as they govern the church

The duties of an apostolic elder are fulfilled by:
- Providing prayerful thought and input on issues before the church, as requested
- Giving strategic input to the church when asked by the senior pastor
- Participating in one retreat/meeting per year, as initiated by the senior pastor

- Resolving disputes that cannot be resolved within the elder body or between the Gateway Church elders and the congregation, at the request of the senior pastor or an individual elder
- Relating to the elder body of Gateway Church as a godly voice of wisdom and counsel

The statement regarding apostolic elders in our bylaws does not undermine the authority of the elders but is built on a relational foundation of trust. In that sense, it is not intrusive into the operations of the organization; rather, it operates through the elders. This allows the apostolic elders to provide a covering and serve as an accountability resource to the organization. If they have a concern with the administration of the ministry, they express it to the elders for discussion that leads to action within the organization.

As part of accountability, we keep the apostolic elders informed about the financial and operational health of the organization. Two regular reports we give to the apostolic elders are:

- Monthly elder minutes for review and information
- Monthly financial statements

We also provide them with any other information they request so that they can be informed and fulfill their apostolic oversight role.

Trans-local Accountability

Key Thought

God gives us as much authority as we are under authority as individuals and as an organization. How can we lead with authority apart from a structure that provides relational oversight and accountability? At Gateway Church, we concluded that we cannot, so we sought a way to establish oversight and accountability apart from a denominational structure.

Summary

This chapter discusses the establishment of external accountability through apostolic influence:
- What are the functions and duties of apostolic elders?
- How are the functions and duties of apostolic elders carried out?

Group Opener

Is the concept of accountability through apostolic elders a conversation our church needs to have?

Group Questions

1. Our senior pastor and elders hold our church staff accountable, but who holds the senior pastor and elders accountable?
2. How well does our outside accountability meet spiritual and relational criteria?
3. How does our outside accountability serve as a support for our senior pastor as he leads and for the elders as they govern?
4. In what ways does our outside accountability help us to resolve disputes that cannot be resolved by the senior pastor and elders?
5. How does our outside accountability serve as a covering during times of crises?
6. Is our outside accountability a regular presence in our church and vested with authority to speak into the life of our congregation? Explain.

Challenge

In the days and weeks ahead, begin to explore on a deep level the lines of accountability and covering over your church. If you determine that a proper covering is not in place, begin to seek God together for the right apostolic elders to provide covering and oversight.

Prayer

Father, we pray that Your Holy Spirit would reveal to us the proper structure of accountability and covering for our church. We want Your blessing, and we know that it comes to those who are submitted to and covered by godly authority. Speak to us, Lord. In Jesus' name, Amen.

Section 4

Building the Organization
We Want

Chapter Eleven

Design and Operation

As CRITICAL AS the work of governance is for fulfilling God's plan for the church, governance alone is not enough. The organizational structure and design of the church and its many ministries play an equally important role. Governance and organizational structure correspond to the level of the church's health. A healthy church must include strategic organizational design for optimal operation. No church can achieve its full impact, grow to its largest capacity, nor develop the full scope of God-given ministry without a structure of organization that allows for efficient ministry. Structure for oversight and reporting within the organization are critical. They help the church maintain a healthy tension between organizational design for individuals in the organization and organizational reporting and accountability. It takes effective organization to run the ministry and produce results.

As the organization grows, its design and operational structure must develop and change. The interface among all the individuals within the ministry must work seamlessly. The senior pastor leads, the elders govern, and the staff and volunteers run the operation of the ministry.

131

The Holy Spirit brings power to the church but to use this power effectively, the church must have structural clarity for unity to have its fruitful effect.

The apostle Paul writes:

But everything should be done in a fitting and orderly way (1 Corinthians 14:40 NIV).

In this verse, Paul outlines the way spiritual gifts should operate in the church. They are the tools that God has given for effective ministry. Paul concludes by saying that the church should do everything, including using gifts, in a fitting and orderly way.

The structure and processes of the ministry organization and operations should reflect the values, policies, and principles held by the church. The efficient operation of the organization should involve a process that implements and reflects the vision of the church.

> *The structure and processes of the ministry organization and operations should reflect the values, policies, and principles held by the church.*

The unity expressed through the governance and structure produces a synergy with ministry, allowing for God's fullest and best result. The psalmist writes:

How good and pleasant it is
For brothers to dwell together in unity!
For there the Lord commanded the blessing;
life forever (Psalm 133:1, 3 NASB).

Every organization should have clearly defined and stated values and principles by which it operates. Early in its development, Gateway Church outlined twelve guiding principles for the operation of ministry. They form the tracks that allow the organization to move forward with clarity and focus.

A standard of excellence: We will reflect the excellence of God in all we do.

We desire to represent God with a heart of excellence in everything we do. We distinguish excellence from perfection or extravagance. Excellence is a heart-attitude that is committed to doing the best with what we have been given, regardless of the scope of the impact or the size of the audience. Excellence leads us to prepare well, prioritize effectively, and focus on God rather than any personal notoriety we may receive from the things we do.

> Keep your behavior excellent among the Gentiles, so that in the thing in which they slander you as evildoers, they may because of your good deeds, as they observe *them*, glorify God in the day of visitation (1 Peter 2:12 NASB).

We are a church, not a movement: We will major in biblical essentials.

God uses movements to highlight or reintroduce a concentrated form of a truth that the church has lost or ignored. Undeniably, God is involved in the movement, and life-changing ministry flows from the highlighted truth. However, a movement cannot highlight a truth and also function in full expression as a church. Movements often start in churches, but sole focus on the movement can cause the church to lose its ability to sustain its base of ministries that train and disciple people.

A movement's singular focus can infuse a scriptural truth into the church that is sweet, right, and life changing, but it will not cover all of the church's needs. It is like a sugar rush from a delicious dessert. It is amazing and memorable, but it cannot sustain the health of the body for a lifetime.

> Then they *began* laying their hands on them, and they were receiving the Holy Spirit. Now when Simon saw that the Spirit was bestowed through the laying on of the apostles' hands, he offered them money, saying, "Give this authority to me as well, so that everyone on whom I lay my hands may receive the Holy Spirit." But Peter said to him, "May your silver perish with you, because you thought you could obtain the gift of God with money! You have no part or portion in this matter, for your heart is not right before God" (Acts 8:17–21 NASB).

We practice proactive problem solving and oversight: *Relationships matter.*

We will not ignore problems just because addressing them would create an uncomfortable situation for the person at the source of the problem or for us. Nor will we allow coping mechanisms to be built as workarounds to avoid honestly and proactively addressing a person or a problem.

You have heard that the ancients were told, "YOU
SHALL NOT COMMIT MURDER" and "Whoever
commits murder shall be liable to the court." But
I say to you that everyone who is angry with his
brother shall be guilty before the court; and whoever
says to his brother, "You good-for-nothing," shall be
guilty before the supreme court; and whoever says,
"You fool," shall be guilty *enough to go* into the fiery
hell. Therefore if you are presenting your offering
at the altar, and there remember that your brother
has something against you, leave your offering there
before the altar and go; first be reconciled to your
brother, and then come and present your offering
(Matthew 5:21–24 NASB).

*We submit to authority and walk in accountability
under recognized authority.*

We will each recognize that God has established
authority, and He is the one who ultimately appoints
people to positions of authority. We affirm that Scripture
categorizes rebellion as an act similar to witchcraft. We
recognize that God works through authority, so we will
submit to authority and walk in accountability to the
authority under which God has put us. *We believe that
you will have as much authority in your life as you are
under.*

Every person is to be in subjection to the governing
authorities. For there is no authority except from
God, and those which exist are established by God
(Romans 13:1 NASB).

We prioritize God's direction over administration.

We affirm the importance of administration, planning, and personal experience as resources that provide wisdom for us as far as they help us implement the vision and serve people through the ministry. We recognize that these important resources assist and make ministry more efficient.

The strategic efforts of people whom God has gifted in administration are vital for the effective work of ministry. Policies, procedures, systems of operation, and financial planning are expressions of the administrative ministry at work in the church. These administrative gifts are tremendous servants but incomplete masters for directing the outcome of decisions. The focus of ministry must remain on God, and those in leadership must put their focus on Him. Their effort must first be to hear His voice, believe His direction, and obey His commands. If the focus centers on obedience to God through organizational efforts, then it will not conflict with the other administrative services that support the church.

> And God has appointed in the church, first apostles, second prophets, third teachers, then miracles, then gifts of healings, helps, administrations, *various* kinds of tongues. All are not apostles, are they? All are not prophets, are they? All are not teachers, are they? All are not *workers of* miracles, are they? All do not have gifts of healings, do they? All do not speak with tongues, do they? All do not interpret, do they? But earnestly desire the greater

gifts. And I show you a still more excellent way
(1 Corinthians 12:28–31 NASB).

We believe in justice and will provide equity in employment and compensation.

God is just, and His kingdom operates with fairness. We will seek, in all our business dealings and employee relations, to conduct ourselves with fairness, equity, and integrity.

> The elders who rule well are to be considered worthy of double honor, especially those who work hard at preaching and teaching. For the Scripture says, "YOU SHALL NOT MUZZLE THE OX WHILE HE IS THRESHING," and "The laborer is worthy of his wages" (1 Timothy 5:17–18 NASB).

We value a servant spirit and humility over giftedness.

Jesus modeled servant leadership and declared that the greatest in His kingdom would be the servant of all. We place people in leadership and promote individuals who reflect a willingness to serve with a heart of humility. We will mentor, coach, and promote people who are less gifted but carry themselves with a servant's heart of humility over those who are more gifted but expect other people to serve them and exhibit pride regarding their abilities. We strongly believe that character matters to God, and therefore, it matters to us.

> "But the greatest among you shall be your servant" (Matthew 23:11 NASB).

The expression of your giftedness will rise to the level your character can support.

We will model and mentor health in our personal life.

We will seek to live and reflect a life built on biblical foundations. We will prioritize our personal relationship with God and the quality of our marriage and family relationships before platform ministry. We will demonstrate, in real terms, a love for God, our spouse, our children, and others, recognizing that it is through this reflection that people will know we are followers of Christ. We will model this for those under our oversight, and we will mentor them in these priorities for their own lives and ministries. We believe that honoring the Sabbath is foundational for personal health and a command that God has not removed but remains for those who follow Him. Therefore, we practice and encourage two days off per week, with one of those days recognized as a Sabbath day.

> An overseer, then, must be above reproach, the husband of one wife, temperate, prudent, respectable, hospitable, able to teach, not addicted to wine or pugnacious, but gentle, peaceable, free from the love of money. *He must be* one who manages his own household well, keeping his children under control with all dignity (but if a man does not know how to manage his own household, how will he take care of the church of God?) (1 Timothy 3:2–5 NLT).

We will practice integrity in time and personal energy management.

138

We believe that we must steward our lives and our energy along with our financial resources. We will manage the pace of our activities and commitments, along with timeliness, through behavior that reflects God's character working in us. We acknowledge that we must manage our emotional life. Beyond physical and spiritual health, we must protect and manage our emotional health because it influences the condition of our hearts. We recognize that the heart is the seedbed of our thinking, will, and desires. Therefore, we will not ignore the emotional gauge of our life; rather, we will seek to live and walk in God's rest.

> I will ponder the way that is blameless.
> Oh, when will you come to me?
> I will walk with integrity of heart
> within my house; I will not set before my eyes
> anything that is worthless.
> I hate the work of those who fall away;
> it shall not cling to me.
> A perverse heart shall be far from me;
> I will know nothing of evil (Psalm 101:2–4 ESV).

We will lead and minister with the authority of the Holy Spirit.

We minister from a place of service and with an attitude of service rather than focusing on self-promotion. When God places us in a position of authority, we will not arrogantly lord it over others but will use it to serve those who work with us and other people. We also will not apologize for or abdicate our leadership to others, nor will we withhold our perspectives on issues simply because someone else has a strong personality or opinion. We will minister with humility, yet with confidence, because God has appointed us to the position we hold, and we depend upon the Holy Spirit enabling us to do our work effectively.

> If you put these things before the brothers, you will be a good servant of Christ Jesus, being trained in the words of the faith and of the good doctrine that you have followed. Have nothing to do with irreverent, silly myths. Rather train yourself for godliness; for while bodily training is of some value, godliness is of value in every way, as it holds promise for the present life and also for the life to come. The saying is trustworthy and deserving of full acceptance. For to this end we toil and strive, because we have our hope set on the living God, who is the Savior of all people, especially of those who believe.
>
> Command and teach these things. Let no one despise you for your youth, but set the believers an example in speech, in conduct, in love, in faith, in purity. Until I come, devote yourself to the public reading of Scripture, to exhortation, to teaching (1 Timothy 4:6–13 ESV).

We will honor the Sabbath and protect rest as an expression of health.

God does not intend for His work to become all-consuming. Jesus told us that His responsibilities are easy and His burden is light. We will work hard but also honor God with a day to stop our work responsibilities and allow ourselves to be renewed and refreshed.

Remember the Sabbath day, to keep it holy. Six days you shall labor, and do all your work, but the seventh day is a Sabbath to the Lord your God. On it you shall not do any work, you, or your son, or your daughter, your male servant, or your female servant, or your livestock, or the sojourner who is within your gates. For in six days the Lord made heaven and earth, the sea, and all that is in them, and rested on the seventh day. Therefore the Lord blessed the Sabbath day and made it holy (Exodus 20:8–11 ESV).

We will live and demonstrate personal qualities of character and morality.

Our personal lives as believers reflect our intimacy with and devotion to God. We will not separate our ministry service responsibilities from our devotion to and intimacy with God. We will reflect God's nature and seek to express His character in our lives. The fruit of God's Spirit includes love, joy, peace, patience, kindness, goodness, faithfulness, gentleness, and self-control. Therefore, our purpose is to reflect the qualities of this fruit through our behavior so that others see them consistently in every area of our lives.

His divine power has granted to us all things that pertain to life and godliness, through the knowledge of him who called us to his own glory and excellence, by which he has granted to us his precious and very great promises, so that through them you may become partakers of the divine nature, having escaped from the corruption that is in the world because of sinful desire. For this very reason, make every effort to supplement your faith with virtue, and virtue with knowledge, and knowledge with self-control, and self-control with steadfastness, and steadfastness with godliness, and godliness with brotherly affection, and brotherly affection with love. For if these qualities are yours and are increasing, they keep you from being ineffective or unfruitful in the knowledge of our Lord Jesus Christ (2 Peter 1:3–8 ESV).

Chapter Eleven Study Guide

Design and Operation

Key Thought

As critical as the work of governance is for fulfilling God's plan for the church, it alone is not enough. The organizational structure and design of the church and its many ministries play an equally important role. Governance and organizational structure correspond to the level of the church's health. A healthy church must include strategic organizational design for optimal operation.

Summary

This chapter discusses the clearly defined and stated principles on which Gateway Church is structured. These twelve principles include:

- A standard of excellence: We will reflect the excellence of God in all we do.
- We are a church, not a movement: We will major in biblical essentials.
- We practice proactive problem solving and oversight: Relationships matter.

- We submit to authority and walk in accountability under recognized authority.
- We prioritize God's direction over administration.
- We believe in justice and will provide equity in employment and compensation.
- We value a servant spirit and humility over giftedness.
- We will model and mentor health in our personal life.
- We will practice integrity in time and personal energy management.
- We will lead and minister with the authority of the Holy Spirit.
- We will honor the Sabbath and protect rest as an expression of health.
- We will live and demonstrate personal qualities of character and morality.

Group Opener

Up to this point, we have only discussed church government. Begin to explore the principles that directly affect the organizational structure of your church.

Group Questions

1. Does our church have a clearly defined and stated set of principles by which it operates? Explain.
2. How are those principles clearly seen in the structure of our church?
3. How are the principles and structure of our church clearly communicated to our staff and congregation?

4. What are the structural problems that exist because our church has not communicated its principles?
5. What are some ways that we can begin to state our principles clearly and implement them into our structure?
6. What are some areas that would be positively affected by clearly stated and implemented principles?

Challenge

In the days and weeks ahead, explore on a deep level the guiding principles of your church. Identify where your structure does not reflect those principles and begin to make the right changes in a healthy way.

Prayer

Father, we want Your principles to be the foundation of our church structure. Give us the grace to discover what You are saying and the strength to make the right adjustments. In Jesus' name, Amen.

Chapter Twelve

Culture

ALL ORGANIZATIONS, INSTITUTIONS, and families have a culture. Some approach the matter with more intent in their identification and protection of their culture than others, but regardless of how intentional you are in establishing and protecting your culture, it still exists. Culture refers to the accepted beliefs, values, attitudes, goals, hierarchies of interaction, and normal practices acquired by a group of people through experience, individual interaction, and group influence. Culture is the tangible expression of who we are individually and as a group. Therefore, the development, expression, and protection of our culture are important and worthwhile processes for us to engage in as an organization and a family. Culture becomes the accepted way to conduct life for a group of people—it is the behaviors, practices, habits, beliefs, values, and symbols the group accepts, generally without thinking about them. These are passed along by communication and imitation from one person to another and one generation to the next.

Some groups do not value or protect culture because they want to include all people, regardless of differences in individual values, attitudes, beliefs, and normal practices.

Under the guise of acceptance of "all," they sacrifice their unique expression, which is their culture. When they do not intentionally preserve their culture, their identity is at risk. If culture can be changed or influenced by every new person and idea that come into the ministry, conflict will arise when people with new values seek to replace the church's standing values. The conflict over the values that will be the group's expression escalates, and the church finds itself in the middle of a *culture war*. Culture wars are efforts, conflicts, and disagreements that occur when new values, beliefs, attitudes, and practices threaten the way the members of a church interact and conduct their lives.

An organization holds core values that provide the foundation for the development and expression of culture within that organization. At Gateway Church, we have 12 core values at the foundation of our culture from which every part of ministry operates:

UNITY

We do everything in a unified way. We desire to be in unity, which, as I have already mentioned, is not conformity. Unity honestly represents the way we feel. Then, we walk together in support of one another.

EXCELLENCE

In every area of ministry and administration, we want to hold a standard or be a standard-bearer for God's excellence. Every individual will exhibit that same spirit. Excellence is not the same as perfectionism. Instead, it actively embraces a continuous effort to do things better and always strives for God's best. Every person in the ministry, whether they are working in the nursery, teaching students, or delivering a sermon from the pulpit, should aspire to do their very best. We give our very best effort regardless of the group's size. Whether few or many, we do not vary the amount of our effort, the diligence of our preparation, or the excellence of our approach for a project. We do not follow a standard that says, "A lot of people will be there, so I better give it my best" as opposed to "There's just going to be a few people there this time, so I don't have to take it as seriously." We will give our very best every time; that is what excellence does.

HUMILITY

We will do everything with the humble spirit of a servant.

SERVICE

God calls us to demonstrate an attitude of servanthood.

FAITH

The author of Hebrews says:

Without faith *it is* impossible to please *Him,* for he who comes to God must believe that He is, and *that*

He is a rewarder of those who diligently seek Him (Hebrews 11:6).

We want to create a positive, grateful atmosphere. We want people to understand that according to Ephesians 3:20, through reliance on God, we can exceed the capabilities of our own minds and abilities. We desire an environment that communicates that our capability is not based on our bank account or our own abilities. If God says it, we can do it. We work in an atmosphere of faith.

EQUITY

We are committed to justice and the right treatment of all individuals, whether they are staff members, volunteers, or any other person. We care for them as much as we care for ourselves.

COMPASSION

We will express an attitude and spirit of compassion and mercy, balanced with truth, to every person.

SUBMISSION

We embrace God's ultimate position of authority, and we walk in submission to each other with love and a desire for relationship.

INTEGRITY

We uphold all biblical standards for conduct and reputation in personal, family, business, financial, and community involvement for all individuals in the organization. For example, if you are in ministry here, it is important that you pay your bills. It is also important that you conduct yourself in an honorable and righteous fashion in the way that you do business, not just when you are in church or fulfilling a ministry responsibility. You should conduct yourself with integrity when you stand at the airline check-in counter, and your flight has been delayed. You will act with integrity when someone jumps in line in front of you with two cartloads of groceries, and you only have one item. It is not acceptable to succumb to frustration, lose your temper, and then come to Gateway Church and think you can minister. We seek to do things with integrity in every situation.

GENEROSITY

We seek opportunities to share our resources generously and to reproduce what God has produced in and given to us.

KINGDOM-CENTERED

We know that our church is not the only church; we are a part of God's greater kingdom. Many churches do great things, and we want to join God in His work in other places. We do not assume God only works with us. We reject the attitude that "We're going to lead in everything, and we're going to invite people to be a part of us, or else we're not going to be a part." No, we want to be a part of kingdom work, and we do not have to lead every time. We simply want to join with God in His bigger plan.

TRUTH AND SPIRIT-CENTERED

We commit ourselves to being fully grounded in scriptural truth and fully empowered by the Holy Spirit. Every organization must possess and hold each person accountable in order to operate at its most effective level.

These are our values. They influence the way we pay our bills, represent each other and ourselves in different areas of ministry, and hold ourselves and each other accountable. They are essential for ministry and our service to God. These core values are expressed in different ways and have differing depths of expression within our organization. Ultimately, the expressions of these values turn into celebrations of our culture. The culture that develops is expressed and reflected through the symbols, heroes, and rituals that we hold up as the reflection of our values and ultimately influence our practices. The most superficial expression of culture is represented in symbols, while the deepest expression is expressed through our values. In the middle are the heroes and rituals that we lift up as examples of our values and that we demonstrate and celebrate as a group. These are some of the ways that we express our core values:

Symbols are words, gestures, pictures, or objects that carry meaning, which only those who share the same culture can recognize. New symbols easily develop while old ones disappear or fall into disuse. Others regularly copy symbols from another group. Thus, symbols represent the outermost layer of a culture.

Heroes are persons, past or present, real or fictitious, who possess characteristics that are highly prized in a culture. They also serve as exemplars of the faith and models for behavior.

Rituals are the collective practices of the group, both major and minor activities. They form part of the process to achieve the desired objectives. They become so much a part of the process that the group considers them essential for achieving the desired results.

Values form the core of a culture. The group accepts these methods of behavior and applies them to their efforts to produce a result. Absent a strategic intent and a diligent effort to identify and protect these values, as an organization matures over time, they can become unconscious expressions for those who hold them. However, the group may run the risk that new members of the team may not understand nor embrace them. Consequently, leaders must regularly discuss, observe, and celebrate these values. Values must be lived and not merely discussed. If someone's actions are inconsistent with the expressed values, then leaders should question his actions. The leaders should explain the values and expected appropriate behaviors. Every member of the group is held accountable for their expression of the organization's values.

The diagram below illustrates the concentric circles that give context to the way we live our values and how they ultimately become the celebrations of our culture.

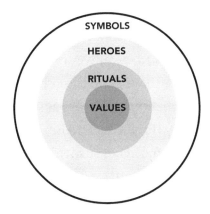

When we consistently express through the symbols, heroes, and rituals within the group, our actions and celebrations serve as the living or pictorial expression of the group's values and ultimately serve as the reflected expressions of the culture. The true cultural meaning of our values is intangible until we give them meaning through their living or pictorial representation. When this representation happens, the values are given context for understanding and for further application as they are interpreted by the group.

Since culture is represented through these various expressions and reflects the values of a group, the group must guard the expressions to make sure that they are not eroded and ultimately lost. Through a process, we have defined and embraced the values that we hold. Their interpretation and application have also followed a process. If we are going to change our values or their application, the change must also follow a process. We should clearly define the process so that we can strategically protect the culture. The group cannot allow its values to be changed simply because new people are absorbed and included who do not hold the same values as the group. In fact, some new people may attempt to insert their own values and fight to replace the group's current values. If they successfully replace the group's values without a process, they have reset the culture. However, the newcomers lack context or awareness of the way those values have been lived out by the group. In addition, everyone in the group will become confused because they have embraced the group's values and cultural expressions that have been quickly or easily changed. They have taken the values as their own but will become confused when new values replace them without a well-defined process.

To protect our culture, we must radically enforce our values and guard them against individual pressure or casual drift. We must vigilantly protect the values we hold, even with the understanding that our ministry methods will change over time and through the generations. As we change our methods, the change should still reflect our values for our culture to remain secure. A new method may add to the visual expression of our values, as reflected in the symbols, heroes, and rituals we hold and celebrate as part of our culture. Thus, a change in method does not necessitate a change in values. The introduction of new methods allows each generation to connect in a relevant way to the values of the group. Although the method is new, if the values remain the same, we protect the culture, and a new generation gains relevant ways to express those values, which multiple generations have passed down.

The first believers in the early church were Jews. When the early church expanded its understanding of the Gospel to include the Gentiles, the decision created a cultural battle. When God established His covenant with the Jews, He symbolized it by the ritual of circumcision. The early church faced the question: "Does the requirement for circumcision apply to the Gentile believers?" Some believers rose up to protect the covenant and its cultural expression through circumcision. They were not going to allow the values and culture to drift without a process. They did not want to trade their acceptance of the Gentile believers for a change to their culture. God established circumcision to represent that value, and He would have to intervene for them to change or amend it.

God began the process with a revelation to the apostle Peter:

> The next day, as they were on their journey and approaching the city, Peter went up on the housetop about the sixth hour to pray. And he became hungry and wanted something to eat, but while they were preparing it, he fell into a trance and saw the heavens opened and something like a great sheet descending, being let down by its four corners upon the earth. In it were all kinds of animals and reptiles and birds of the air. And there came a voice to him: "Rise, Peter; kill and eat." But Peter said, "By no means, Lord;

for I have never eaten anything that is common
or unclean." And the voice came to him again a
second time, "What God has made clean, do not call
common." This happened three times, and the thing
was taken up at once to heaven (Acts 10:9–16 ESV).

This encounter laid the foundation for Peter's response
and God's work in the lives of Cornelius and his family. It
didn't stop there, however.

The controversy over circumcision as a value and a symbol
continued. Paul disagreed with the believers who resisted and
debated the issue. The issue became so contentious that the
Antioch church dispatched Paul and Barnabas to Jerusalem.
Acts 15 gives the account of that meeting. After much debate,
conferring with the Scriptures, and hearing from everyone
who had anything to say, the council concluded:

After they finished speaking, James replied,
"Brothers, listen to me. Simeon has related how God
first visited the Gentiles, to take from them a people
for his name. And with this the words of the prophets
agree, just as it is written,

'After this I will return,
and I will rebuild the tent of David that has fallen;
I will rebuild its ruins,
and I will restore it,
that the remnant of mankind may seek the Lord,
and all the Gentiles who are called by my name,
says the Lord, who makes these things known
  from of old.'

Therefore my judgment is that we should not trouble those of the Gentiles who turn to God, but should write to them to abstain from the things polluted by idols, and from sexual immorality, and from what has been strangled, and from blood. For from ancient generations Moses has had in every city those who proclaim him, for he is read every Sabbath in the synagogues."

Then it seemed good to the apostles and the elders, with the whole church, to choose men from among them and send them to Antioch with Paul and Barnabas. They sent Judas called Barsabbas, and Silas, leading men among the brothers, with the following letter: "The brothers, both the apostles and the elders, to the brothers who are of the Gentiles in Antioch and Syria and Cilicia, greetings. Since we have heard that some persons have gone out from us and troubled you with words, unsettling your minds, although we gave them no instructions, it has seemed good to us, having come to one accord, to choose men and send them to you with our beloved Barnabas and Paul, men who have risked their lives for the name of our Lord Jesus Christ. We have therefore sent Judas and Silas, who themselves will tell you the same things by word of mouth. For it has seemed good to the Holy Spirit and to us to lay on you no greater burden than these requirements: that you abstain from what has been sacrificed to idols, and from blood, and from what has been strangled, and from sexual immorality. If you keep yourselves from these, you will do well. Farewell" (Acts 15:13–29 ESV).

A church should vigorously protect its culture and only change it through a defined process under the leadership of the Holy Spirit.

Chapter Twelve Study Guide

Culture

Key Thought

Culture is the tangible expression of who we are individually and as a group. Therefore, the development, expression, and protection of our culture are important and worthwhile processes for our organization. Culture becomes the accepted way to conduct life for a group of people—it is the behaviors, practices, habits, beliefs, values, and symbols the group accepts, generally without thinking about them. These are passed along by communication and imitation from one person to another and one generation to the next.

Summary

This chapter discusses the core values upon which Gateway Church's culture is founded. These values, listed below, are expressed through symbols, heroes, and rituals.

- Unity
- Excellence

- Humility
- Service
- Faith
- Equity
- Compassion
- Submission
- Integrity
- Generosity
- Kingdom-centered
- Truth and Spirit-centered

Group Opener

In this chapter, we asked questions about values. Begin to explore how your church's values directly affect the culture of your church.

Group Questions

1. Does our church have a clearly defined and stated set of values by which it operates? If so, what are they?
2. How are those values seen in the culture of our church?
3. How are the values of our church clearly communicated to our staff and congregation?
4. Are there cultural problems in our church that may exist due to a lack of communication of our values? If so, what are they?
5. What are some ways that we can begin to state our values more clearly and implement them through our culture?

6. What are some areas that would be improved by clearly stated and implemented values?

Challenge

In the days and weeks ahead, begin to explore on a deep level the values of your church. Identify where your culture does not reflect those values and begin to make changes in a healthy way.

Prayer

Father, we want Your values to be at the very foundation of our church culture. Give us the grace to discover what Your Holy Spirit is saying to us and give us the strength to make the right moves. In Jesus' name, Amen.

Chapter Thirteen

Separate Roles for Governing & Oversight

As I MENTIONED in Chapter Three, we describe the separation of responsibilities in our leadership structure in this way: *we are elder governed, senior pastor led, staff and volunteer run, and congregation owned.* Organizational design requires a separation of governing roles from those of operating the organization, overseeing the staff, and implementing the vision. Organizational structure and oversight focus on the roles and responsibilities for overseeing and directing the day-to-day ministry operations, defined by job descriptions and an organizational reporting structure. This chapter and the next summarize how Gateway Church combines these various functions to create a cohesive, healthy structure for governing and operating the church, one which functions on the foundational concepts of theocratic rule and a balance of headship and team leadership.

The Governing Role

The elders govern the church. Governing involves the defining, refining, confirming, and overseeing of the vision, direction, and values of the ministry. As I mentioned previously, the governing function requires an ability to grasp and perceive the breadth of the work God has assigned to us. It maintains a perspective of God's work and orchestrates things from a 30,000-foot view. We define governing in this way:

> Governing confirms the scope of ministry and clarifies the vision of the ministry that the senior pastor establishes. The elders come underneath the visionary expression of the senior pastor to work out, give detail, and confirm the vision that he has established. They monitor the ministry results and ensure successful fulfillment of the vision. The elders evaluate the condition of the ministry by monitoring its results. They work to support the implementation of ministry by the staff through respecting the church's organizational structure. For the elders to govern effectively, they must have reporting mechanisms that give them accurate and timely information to monitor and evaluate the results. The validity and accuracy of those reports are critical to their governing function. The elders have the responsibility to establish the timing for major ministry initiatives within the church. They work in partnership with the staff to establish the emphasis, priorities, and timing for implementation of the major initiatives, and they provide the accountable covering for the church's major decisions.

The structure of governance affects major decisions. At Gateway Church, we want to determine how to facilitate the ongoing growth of the ministry that God has given to us. Several years ago, we started to outgrow our facility. We already conducted multiple worship services, so the elders determined it was time to begin looking for new property. Timing is critical in decisions of this type. The elder body made the decision to look for property, established the timing, and determined the size of property that we needed. Our facility (and only campus) at the time was on 15 acres in Southlake. The elders decided that we needed a piece of property around 60 acres in size to accommodate our growing church at its current size and into the future. This decision was influenced by the broad vision of the senior pastor and what God had impressed upon him for the future of Gateway Church.

The elders empowered another leader and me to begin the search. The elders gave us the parameters for negotiations. We reported to them about the properties we found and their cost. Then the elders decided to focus on one piece of property. They set the criteria for the offering price and purchase conditions, which empowered us to move forward with negotiations. It was a partnership between the governing of the church by the elders and the operating of the church by the staff. The scope and timing of decisions, such as building and expanding, are parts of the governing function of the elders.

The elders also establish the financial authority and boundaries for the staff to operate within. They are responsible for approving the annual budget, determining the salary ranges of the job categories, and setting the spending limits for non-budgeted items. They approve and monitor the number of overall staff, but they do not make specific staff hiring decisions. The elders set the amount of annual pay increases for the staff as part of the budgeting process. This practice does not constrain the organization. Instead, it produces accountability, which is a healthy part of the operation of the organization of the church.

Every person on staff at Gateway Church falls into a job category with a pay scale. Every position has an entry, mid-range, and maximum salary. When we interview someone for a position, we know into what category the position falls, which defines the salary range for us to discuss with the job candidate. The governance process provides the tools for the organization to do its part in filling employment needs by clearly defining the hiring manager's authority for negotiating with the candidate. With these guidelines in place, hiring managers do not have to ask the elders' permission to hire the necessary staff if the salary is within the range and fits within the approved personnel budget. Under these parameters, the organization is empowered to act. The elders' governing function establishes the financial boundaries that give the organization the authority to operate the ministry with spiritual authority and power. The elders teach, minister, pray for the sick, and express their individual passions for ministry within the organization. As they minister, the elders provide an example of godly character and leadership to the body.

Operational Role

Staff and volunteers make up the organization. They are responsible for implementing the vision and daily running the ministry. The partnership between the governing elders and the organization's structure of staff and volunteers operating the ministry is not in conflict; rather, it is respectful and mutually supportive. The ministry could not move forward without an army of volunteers. The staff assumes the role of training, recruiting, and equipping the volunteers for the work of ministry. This role is what the apostle Paul describes in Ephesians:

> And he gave the apostles, the prophets, the evangelists, the shepherds and teachers, to equip the saints for the work of ministry, for building up the body of Christ (4:11–12 ESV).

Our staff conducts ministry as an expression of their function to train and equip. I will expand upon this in the next chapter.

Congregational Ownership

Gateway Church is congregation owned, which means that the congregation owns the assets of the organization, and the elders and staff manage them on their behalf. We have a fiduciary responsibility to the congregation. We deliver the results in an annual report to the congregation. At one time, we held an annual business meeting. Over time, we have found that delivering annual audited financial statements and a detailed report of the results of the ministry through a website and at special weekend services was a more effective way to inform the congregation.

Since the congregation owns the assets, we come to the congregation to vote on the purchase or sale of substantial amounts of real property or assets. Since the beginning of the ministry, we have defined substantial as an amount greater than 10% of our net assets. By defining it that way, the amount is scalable with our growth. It also means we have empowered the organization to conduct business without a large number of votes.

In fact, there are only two reasons we take a congregational vote: (1) when the purchase amount is greater than 10% of our net assets and (2) when we are launching or increasing the scope of our vision and ministry expression. As an example, when we purchased the property for our Southlake campus, it was 190 acres, and the cost of the project was more than the 10% threshold. However, the purchase also represented the launch of an increased scope of ministry. Consequently, we sought the approval and confirmation for both the purchase and the increased scope of vision and ministry expression. As such, the vote included both approval and affirmation. Both reasons were important to the elders and staff as we moved forward with the property, which we now use as our primary broadcast campus that serves all our campuses on the weekends.

Separate Roles for Governing & Oversight

Key Thought

Organizational design requires a separation of governing roles from those of operating the organization, overseeing the staff, and implementing the vision. Organizational structure and oversight focus on the roles and responsibilities for the oversight and direction of the day-to-day ministry operations, defined by job descriptions and an organizational reporting structure. Gateway Church combines the various functions of governing and operating to create a cohesive, healthy structure.

Summary

This chapter clearly defines the governing role as separate from the operational role. The elders govern by defining, refining, confirming, and overseeing the vision, direction, and values of the ministry. The staff and volunteers fulfill the operational role by implementing the vision and running the day-to-day ministry. Together, the elders, staff, and volunteers manage the assets of the organization, which are owned by the congregation.

Group Opener

The separation of roles may be a new concept, or it may require deeper discussion. Consider the following questions about the governing and operational roles of your church.

Group Questions

1. How is the scope and timing of major projects and vision determined in our church? Is this elder driven, or do we follow some other model?
2. How does our church determine financial authority and boundaries for the staff? Is this elder driven, or do we follow some other model?
3. How are ministry results monitored to ensure fulfillment of the vision? Is this elder driven, or we follow some other model?
4. Is there a reporting mechanism in place? If so, does the mechanism lead back to inform the elders?
5. Do the staff members have the tools they need to do the work of the ministry? Who defines and provides these tools?
6. What are the areas in our church that require the governing of the elders?
7. What are the areas in our church that require support for the daily operations of the ministry?

Challenge

In the days and weeks ahead, explore on a deep level the areas where the separation of roles is required. Begin to strategize about matters of governing that can be put into the hands of the elders and ways to empower the staff and volunteers so that the church can function in a healthy manner.

Prayer

Father, we ask You to give us eyes to see which areas in our church are matters of government and which are matters of operation. We ask You to give us the grace to set things in the proper place so that health can come to our church. In Jesus' name, Amen.

Chapter Fourteen

Relational Oversight

STAFF AND VOLUNTEERS comprise the organization to conduct the ministry of Gateway Church. Ministry is the collective expression of the individual efforts within a group or organization as we serve God and people. Ministry is an inclusive term—it means everything represented and produced by the efforts of the staff and volunteers of Gateway Church. The oversight structure exists to implement the vision, support the expression of ministry, and oversee the work to ensure effective results.

Ministry leaders may be effective, focused, and completely immersed in the work of their assigned area. However, with their heads lowered and minds laser-focused, they cannot know about every area of the ministry. Consequently, the executive leadership must connect all the parts, which enables the staff to focus on their areas without assuming responsibility for the entire organization. It also enables oversight to monitor ministry pace and its impact on each individual. This is what we call relational oversight.

We do not expect every staff member to understand all areas of ministry; the scope is too great. The executive leaders maintain overarching responsibility for church operations. The departmental staff members focus on specific areas and use their expertise to further the work in those areas. At Gateway Church, the senior pastor is the executive leader of the church. He works with and empowers an executive team that enables him to guide the organization to implement the vision and minister to the congregation.

The Senior Pastor's Role in Oversight

Previously, I addressed the qualifications for the senior pastor, but now I want to discuss his leadership role in the organization. Concerning his leading, the senior pastor must guide the organization as it implements the vision. His leadership inspires, clarifies, and sets in their proper place the individuals needed to implement the vision for the ministry. His leadership also motivates and guides the organization, as well as the congregation, as he points each toward fulfillment of the vision. He establishes and protects the values of the organization and monitors their expression through the operation of the ministry.

Some time ago, I had a conversation with Pastor Robert about a situation that had developed within the organization. He addressed it by saying that it did not represent our values. Then, he specifically referred to one of our core values mentioned in Chapter Twelve. He asked, "How does that reflect this value?" I answered, "I agree with you—it doesn't." Next, he asked, "What are we going to do about that?" I replied, "We're going to bring it in line with our values." And we did just that. We changed it to reflect our culture and who we are.

The senior pastor has the responsibility to make sure that the elders, staff, and volunteers are living true to the values and cultural principles of the church and that they flow through the entire organization. As the head of the organization, he provides the connective link between the staff and volunteers and the elders. Since he is the singular head of the church, chairman of the elders, chief executive of the organization, and senior pastor of the congregation, he makes sure that the expression of the church's vision and values remains consistent throughout every level of the organization and in all implementations of ministry. He is responsible to the elders as he leads the staff and feeds the congregation through biblical preaching and teaching. He feeds from the Word of God and leads from revelation received through prayer.

From my vantage point as a member of the executive team, no voice carries greater authority and respect in our organization than that of Pastor Robert. As the senior pastor, God has set him in such a role that when he instructs, leads, and casts vision, it carries weight that comes from heaven itself. Since heaven's authority rests on him as the person that God put in place, it is his responsibility to lead. There cannot be a leadership void. The senior pastor must provide leadership to the multiple expressions of the ministry. God empowers and anoints him to do so.

If I Could Speak a Word to Senior Pastors . . .

I encourage you to lead with confidence and depend upon the Holy Spirit. I ask you not to give up your leadership role. It is not something that you may hold with arrogance; however, neither can you act with false humility. Failing to fulfill your responsibility out of the belief that you should be a passive leader and allow someone else to lead does not help the organization. You should not have to defend your responsibility to lead nor feel the need to fight to establish it. God gave it to you, so lead with humility and authority. The elders, staff, volunteers, and congregation need you to fulfill your God-appointed role.

Requirements for Ministry Service

Positions of ministry service are open to all believers, based on their commitment to God, their commitment to the church (including its membership and vision), and their willingness to submit to the structure of authority that is in place. We believe that God directs people into ministry in response to their love and service to Him, so we embrace the anointing of God on all believers for the expression of their gifts and service. We ask those who serve in our church (including all employees) to first become members of the church. As they come into membership, they express their commitment to God's work through our church. If they are going to find a place of service, they first need to have exposure to the vision that God has given Gateway Church.

They need to be committed believers who have willingly chosen to support the vision of the ministry with their time, talents, and resources. Ministry service is just that— it is a place of service. We take it seriously and ask those who serve to do the same. Our desire is to serve God and His kingdom. As such, we want those who serve to be growing, passionate, maturing believers.

Women in Ministry

Regarding the ministry role of women at Gateway Church, we believe God anoints and appoints both men and women to positions of ministry. We believe that God has gifted women just as He has men. We believe God calls women to vocational service just as He calls men. The only place where we limit the service of women is in positions of ultimate headship. Therefore, the roles of elder and senior pastor would not be open to women because we believe these are male-only leadership roles.

We believe that women have every gifting, ability, and anointing God has given to men. However, from a biblical perspective, we believe that the authority to govern is the responsibility of the senior pastor and the elders. These positions are the expression of ultimate headship in our understanding of ministry. Over several years, as I have taught about this matter, I have found overwhelming support and agreement among both men and women, in part because our position does not demean women. We love, respect, and honor women and provide them roles in ministry service that are equal to those of men.

The most common response I hear from women as I present Gateway Church's perspective on their place of service is that they agree and do not want a position of final authority and responsibility to lead the church. They want respect and validation, which we seek to give them in multiple ways. With respect and validation, they are satisfied to fulfill significant roles that fit within the organization but are not positions of ultimate headship. We give women opportunities to use their gifts to serve God and people, and we benefit from their service.

Some might say, "Don't you know the history of Israel and the Church?" We know that Deborah served as a judge in Israel. We have read about Esther, the queen who saved the Hebrew people from annihilation. We remember Kathryn Kuhlman and Aimee Semple McPherson. No doubt, these godly women led and were used by God. Others may not agree, but we believe that when women have filled the role of governing (a role that I submit God wanted to fill with men), it was because men abdicated their responsibility to govern. Isn't this what happened between Deborah and Barak?

> Now Deborah, a prophetess, the wife of Lappidoth, was judging Israel at that time. She used to sit under the palm of Deborah between Ramah and Bethel in the hill country of Ephraim, and the people of Israel came up to her for judgment. She sent and summoned Barak the son of Abinoam from Kedesh-naphtali and said to him, "Has not the Lord, the God of Israel, commanded you, 'Go, gather your men at Mount Tabor, taking 10,000 from the people of Naphtali and the people of Zebulun. And I will draw out Sisera,

the general of Jabin's army, to meet you by the river Kishon with his chariots and his troops, and I will give him into your hand'?" Barak said to her, "If you will go with me, I will go, but if you will not go with me, I will not go." And she said, "I will surely go with you. Nevertheless, the road on which you are going will not lead to your glory, for the Lord will sell Sisera into the hand of a woman." Then Deborah arose and went with Barak to Kedesh (Judges 4:4–9 ESV).

As I have said, women can express every gift and ability to teach, lead, and serve as God empowers them, including vocational ministry. At Gateway Church, the only ministry limitation for women relates to the governmental function. We will not consider them to fill the senior pastor role, nor to serve as members of the elder body. We do not believe that this takes away from our desire to validate and empower the giftedness of women in ministry; rather, it identifies and confirms their significance and affirms God's call, work, and ministry service for both men and women.

The Role of Leading Staff and Volunteers

God calls every believer to ministry. He assigns some believers to vocational or professional ministry, and others He appoints to volunteer or non-vocational service. God calls staff members and volunteers to work in the church. Their united effort is to proclaim the gospel of Jesus Christ and live out its practical expression through the fulfillment of the vision of the church's ministry and its service to people. They do this work through harmony and partnership under the senior pastor's leadership. God speaks to every believer through both personal vision and corporate vision. We should not confuse those two kinds of vision. When personal vision conflicts with the corporate vision, as defined by the senior pastor and confirmed by the elders, then its fulfillment is not through the church. That conflict can mean that God is moving an individual out of the church or that a personal vision is for another time.

The following is one example to explain why a personal vision cannot override the corporate vision. Several years ago, I developed a proposal for a Christian health club facility. I was very excited about this possibility. I developed the idea while I was still in business. It was particularly attractive to me because I frequently played racquetball. I thought it represented a great opportunity to blend my love for business and for God in a way that would help people. As I planned the launch of this health club, God completely shifted my focus. I exited the secular business environment and entered full-time vocational ministry. In the process of this transition, I sold the business proposal to someone else who built such a facility, and God moved me into vocational ministry. With the health club built, I gave my heart and attention to ministry. Several years later, I learned that the health club was facing financial difficulties and might be for sale.

When I heard this report, I was getting ready to leave for a men's retreat. One of the retreat's sessions dealt with listening to God. At the session, the facilitator told us to write down the things we heard God say. Several hundred men attended the retreat, and we all wrote down things we heard from God. I wrote, "This racquetball/health facility is going to be returned to you for the glory of God, and everything's going to be as I gave you in the original vision; I will be glorified in its use." Then I wrote, "This is going to be for the congregation." These things were flowing, and I was convinced that God was in it. I listened intently and wrote what I heard. After the session, I returned to my room, where I was staying with our senior pastor. I asked him, "Well, did God speak to you?" He said that God had, and he read to me what he had written. It was good. It resonated in my heart. So, I said, "Man, I agree. I think that's God!" Then he asked me, "Well, what did God say to *you*?" So, I read to him what I had written.

When I finished, he said, "Tom, that's not God." I was shocked and a little stunned. I responded, "I said *yours* was God! You're supposed to say *mine* was God too!" Then he said, "No. I can't say it's God if it's not." He continued, "If this is in your heart to do it, then it may be from God, but it is your personal vision. It is not part of the vision of the church to own or run a health facility."

My personal vision cannot amend the church's corporate vision that our senior pastor establishes. As good as my personal vision may be, if I try to connect or equate my personal vision with the church's vision, the corporate vision runs the danger of devolving into a hodgepodge of individual visions instead of God's vision revealed through a godly process. Allowing individual members to say, "Maybe this is what God wants us to do in the community," and attempting to shoehorn it into the corporate vision is not God's plan. The corporate vision comes under the canopy of the senior pastor's singular leadership as he listens to God's voice. The corporate vision is not an amalgamation of individual visions. The confirmation of the elders involves a process to clarify and confirm the skeletal vision of the senior pastor. The church's vision is not the insertion of a vision by an individual member, elder, or key leader. We do not operate as if we are a team of chefs all throwing their favorite ingredients into the pot to create a special dish. Imagine how that dish would taste! Instead, the corporate vision is a process that reflects the preparation of a spiritual multi-course meal by a skilled kitchen staff based on the senior pastor's recipe—his God-given vision.

Equipping Volunteers for the Work of Ministry

Staff members equip and empower the congregation for ministry. According to the apostle Paul, the work of ministry is to prepare and then release people into ministry service for the building up of the church body (Ephesians 4). Consequently, someone might say, "Well, the vocational ministers *do* the ministry, but I am just a member." Some people might see themselves as along for the ride as recipients of ministry but do not engage in ministry service themselves. At Gateway Church, we help our members understand that their maturity and development as believers includes ministry service. We explain and apply Paul's statement to the Ephesians as we work to prepare and then release them to do the ministry.

We show members how to minister as we train them, but we expect them to learn and then do the ministry. The staff members and volunteer leaders focus on training and building systems and processes to assist in ministry development. Through a mentoring model of ministry with a focus on training, our goal is to provide the tools and structure necessary for staff and volunteer members to reproduce ministry. Once we place and train people for ministry, the trainers turn their attention to overseeing those whom they have trained.

Providing Relational Oversight

After empowering the team with recruiting and training, leadership continues with relational oversight, which consists of two parts. It means that staff members commit to meet regularly to review the work as well as ensure that resources are made available for the ministry. Resources include not only money made available through the budget but also people and things, such as additional volunteers, facilities, and equipment for the work.

What is the nature of *relational* oversight? It shows an interest in the well-being of individuals, as well as managing the ministry task. Relational oversight is built on the desire to do ministry together for a long time. We contrast this approach with the desire to get ministry done regardless of the cost. If we focus solely on results, then we will use people until they can no longer perform the needed task. Afterwards, we might discard and replace them with someone else who can do the job at hand. Without question, ministry success requires work, with responsibilities and duties to fulfill. However, we believe that we can achieve success without overworking or discarding people. We can do ministry in a way that does not put the things we hold dear in jeopardy, including our personal relationship with God, our marriages, our families, and our enjoyable lives. Relational oversight includes several simple elements for the oversight structure. We provide training that contains these elements for staff members and volunteers who oversee others.

Regular Meetings

The oversight process establishes a routine that supportively monitors people and projects. Even in the middle of busy schedules, regular meetings give us the ability to interact relationally and involve ourselves with the people we oversee.

Relationally Driven Meetings

We consider *how* people are doing as more important than *what* they are doing. A relational philosophy must start at the top of the organization and flow all the way through it. When I have an oversight meeting, I like to start with some questions that enable me to connect on a personal level with the person I oversee. I might say, "Before we talk about *what* you're doing, let's talk about *how* you're doing." I will ask things like: "How's your family?" "How is your schedule?" "How are you feeling?" "What's the greatest pressure on you right now?" As friendships develop with the people you oversee, you will be able to ask questions and discuss situations with more personal knowledge. I will ask if their children won their ball games, how their date night went last week, or if they enjoyed the movie they went to see. All these questions contribute to the relational component of providing oversight for the people with whom we share our ministry life, and we hope to do so with them for a long time.

Structure

We have an organizational chart that describes the lines of authority and the alignment of our team for efficient ministry. When the organization changes, the organizational chart must reflect those changes. Sometimes people express amazement at the time and effort it takes to keep this current, and a few have even said that we give too much attention to our organizational chart. Alignment matters when we are talking about the efficiency of the organization, and so do reporting authority, roles, and responsibilities.

We want the structure to facilitate oversight, and we want relational oversight of people to empower them for their ministry responsibilities. We tell our team members that we do not intend for organizational structure to create a barrier to developing and maintaining relationships. We want the structure of our organization to help people connect in friendships. The structure exists to define the way we operate within a clearly defined flow of ministry. Each position in the organization has a job description for both staff and volunteer positions. As the ministry has grown, so has our need for trained and committed volunteers. Our ratio of volunteers to staff members is approximately 5 to 1. I do not believe it is a coincidence that the ratio of members to volunteers is also about the same—5 to 1. This statistic dramatically illustrates the reality of the ministry principle that we hold: *People minister to people.*

Every position, both volunteer and vocational, has a job description that defines the duties, expectations, and qualifications necessary for the position. By defining each position, we can give clear goals to the people doing the work and describe what the successful execution of each position requires. The organizational chart gives a pictorial demonstration of how each position fits into the whole, which provides the framework for better oversight in the organization.

The elders provide the organization with approved policies and budgets, established financial limits for expenses, and financial boundaries related to working capital and debt for daily ministry functions. When the elders give final approval to the budget, they empower the organization to act within those financial limits of authority.

The elders set the financial limits of authority based on levels of organizational responsibility. The limits depend on an individual's assigned responsibilities. As the organization has grown in size and financial scope, we have adjusted the limits to maintain efficiency of operation. When we observe a slowdown in decision-making or an imbalance in responsibilities, we propose changes for the elders to review and approve. Once they approve the changes, they empower the organization for its everyday work of overseeing and implementing the vision.

Relational Oversight

Key Thought

We practice relational oversight because we want to do ministry together for a long time. We contrast this approach with the desire to get ministry done regardless of the cost. If we focus solely on results, then we will use people until they can no longer perform the needed task. Afterwards, we might discard and replace them with someone else who can do the job at hand. Ministry success requires work, with responsibilities and duties to fulfill. However, we believe that we can achieve success without overworking or discarding people.

Summary

This chapter discusses the nature and function of relational oversight. It also addresses the various roles of ministry service, both vocational and volunteer, at Gateway Church:

- The senior pastor's role in oversight
- Requirements for ministry service

- Women in ministry
- The role of leading staff and volunteers
- Equipping volunteers for the work of ministry

Group Opener

There are many roles in local church ministry, and all of them are served through relational oversight. The success we are working toward does not come at the expense of people.

Group Questions

1. How does our senior pastor exercise the responsibility of making sure our church is living true to its values and cultural principles?
2. How do women operate in ministry in our church? How do we communicate a biblical balance in the areas of ministry leadership and ultimate headship regarding women?
3. How does our staff engage in the equipping of volunteers for ministry?
4. How does our church leadership show interest in the well-being of our staff members and volunteers as well as in the management of ministry tasks?
5. Do our staff members and volunteers have a consistent connection to oversight through regular meetings?
6. How are our regular meetings relationally-driven?
7. In what areas of our church should relational oversight be strengthened?

Challenge

In the days and weeks ahead, explore on a deep level the areas where relational oversight can be built or improved. Develop a strategy of oversight in all areas of your church so that it can function in a healthy manner.

Prayer

Father, we ask that You reveal the areas where management needs to be infused with relational oversight. Give us a burden for the people we lead so that we will view them the way You do. In Jesus' name, Amen.

Conclusion

Changing Your Style of Government

A CHURCH MUST have a structure that establishes governance, provides operational authority and accountability, and aligns the responsibilities of all its members to be successful. Do not attempt to make changes quickly. Remember that change may not come easily. If you really want to make changes to your style of church government, I suggest two steps to help you adopt and implement changes to your organization's design and structure:

Step One: Develop a Consensus

First, you must develop a positive attitude toward the changes among the church members and staff. Any change can be hard, and attempting to change your style of governance will be one of the hardest things you can do in your organization. You will have to work through layers of nesting, kingdom building, and turf protecting. In some cases, these ways of operating have decades of precedent and tradition. These traditions have worked their way into the mindset as well as the actions of your church. It will take time, patience, and a tenacity that is rooted in obedient faith to shepherd these changes.

I do not say these things to discourage you. I tell you about them so that you can be realistic in your efforts but not discouraged. Change is part of a healthy atmosphere and necessary for growth; things that are growing will change as they develop and mature. Transitions are also part of God's plan. If you are unwilling to change or have an aversion to helping some people move on from the ministry, you will not succeed in leading this effort.

Remember the 10-80-10 principle of change in Chapter Three. In any change, 10% of the people affected will jump on board at the first suggestion of change. They will be all-in with little or no communication. They love change, embrace it, and find energy from it. Another 10% of the people want nothing to do with change. In fact, they would not embrace change if Jesus Himself announced it. No amount of information or time to process will help these people; they will resist and drag their feet all the way. That leaves 80% who love what God is doing, are committed to the work, and will ultimately come along with the change. They just need time and information.

It is good leadership to recognize this principle and work to take as many as possible of the 80% people along with you. Teach, talk, listen to their concerns, answer their questions, and lead them to embrace these changes so that they will become leaders and support you in the change. You must be willing to talk openly about what is motivating the change and focus prayer in this area.

CHANGING YOUR STYLE OF GOVERNMENT

As you take steps to implement change, recognize that you must overcome the natural resistance. You may be tempted to keep certain people in positions, even when God is transitioning them, because you want to minimize the impact of the change. However, you should use the change as a catalyst to move them to another place of service. Also, recognize that life is lived in seasons, and those seasons change. People you oversee, or maybe even you, experience seasons of change. If so, the reality is that transition may need to happen. When fall is over and winter is in the air, it is unhelpful to hold onto the fleeting days of autumn. It is time to embrace the transition into winter. Get your winter clothes out, winterize the lawn equipment, and get ready for cold and snow.

When God is in the process of moving or reassigning someone, we need to understand that it is for their good. It will further God's purpose in their lives. When God is transitioning people to new places, we do not help them, God, or ourselves by holding onto them. We may keep them simply because we think we need them, they have played a critical role in the past, or the conversation will be difficult. We need to support them in the process of their transition and even build an exit ramp so that they can move into God's work in a new place.

Create training and oversight systems that encourage the continual development of your team. As the organization grows, the staffing needs and their functions change, and people need to change with them. Suppose you began a church several years ago with a small group of people. At the beginning stages, all of them were integral to everything that happened. Currently, however, the church has progressed and moved beyond the skill level of some of those people. They simply are not emotionally and spiritually at the level necessary for leading the church in its current period of growth. They are great people who were necessary in the beginning, but they have not kept up with their personal development. We want them to stay as members of the church and honor them for their contributions, but we need to be able to talk with them about a changing role in a new season so that the ministry can continue growing. Of course, you love them and appreciate their contributions, but, in reality, they have not changed along with the church. At this point, you can either develop a way to cope with them and shield them from impeding progress, or you can help them transition to a new role. This decision is one of the hardest aspects of leading a ministry.

Gateway Church is a growing environment, and change is a part of our culture. We are responsible for keeping up with the change. We step into ministry, either vocational or volunteer, because we sense God's call for us to fulfill His purpose for ourselves and Gateway Church. When that call is complete, as defined by us or those who oversee us, we should surrender to God's voice and say, "I just can't do it anymore. I've given everything I have, I've run my race, and it is time for someone else to carry on from here." We need to give ourselves permission to say, "It's time for somebody else to step in. I took it as far as I could, and now I'm ready to hand it off."

It is not wrong to identify someone as having finished their race. They have not failed; in fact, they have succeeded. They have finished! Make sure that you have leaders who are qualified, healthy, and growing in their walk with God, their service, and their leadership. Proactively identify spiritual sickness and treat it at the earliest stages. Small spiritual colds turn into serious spiritual diseases. If left unaddressed and untreated, they develop into a bigger problem with devastating results. We need to deal with these spiritual viruses in the same way that we would physical ones. Ongoing personal spiritual growth is not optional; it is a requirement for leadership. We must lovingly identify those who have stopped growing and spur them on to love and good works. We must love each other as a part of the process. We are not trying to enforce anything legalistically; rather, we are trying to encourage one another and emphasize that personal, spiritual growth is required for all of us in our service to God and people.

Step 2: Plan and Strategize with the End in Mind

The second step to implementing change requires strategic thought. It involves beginning with the end in mind. We must be methodical and intentional about the changes we make. If we think with the end in mind, then we can lay a deeper foundation in one or more areas because we will build future floors upon the current structure. We will regret thinking only in the present. In many ways, the stages of growth in our ministry function like the physical growth of our bodies; we cannot rush it, but we need to anticipate it. Churches go through stages of growth and maturity.

The Developmental Stage

The first stage of growth is *developmental*. At the church's beginning or when it is still small, survival is the key issue. This stage requires all hands on deck to make the ministry function. People connect relationally as they conduct ministry. During this time, because the group is relatively small, everyone knows each other. They understand everybody's heart and honor and appreciate their willingness to sacrifice. The very existence of the church requires that everyone does their part and makes sacrifices to ensure that the work of the ministry happens. During this stage, the vision and values are instinctively defined as the core leadership emerges.

During the developmental stage, people in the church tend to mix up the roles and functions of leading and governing so that the healthy church government model outlined earlier is not clearly observable. If it were understood, it would be helpful to establish a healthy structure at the beginning, but it is not critical. You may not have enough qualified people to do so. At this stage, relationships drive the ministry, which feels good to everyone, as they have a sense that they are connected; everyone is working together, and everything is held in common. God is the focus. People are ministered to and impacted. However, as things grow, change will happen.

Keeping in mind the concept of beginning with the end in mind, here is a quick review: We advocate recognizing and embracing a singular head for the ministry—we believe that God designed that type of structure. However, the singular head should not be domineering in his leadership, nor should the church develop oligarchical rule. For both support and healthy accountability, God surrounds the singular head with a plurality of leadership. In these early stages, churches may not be able to see the separation of duties easily. As a task needs attention, the person closest to it at the time works on it without concerns about lines of authority.

The Structural Formation Stage

The second stage is *structural formation*. At this stage, survival is assured and no longer has top priority; rather, the management of growth and the formation of the systems and structure to facilitate the work of ministry emerge as the central issues. The scope of ministry expands beyond the ability of informal, familial oversight to remain effective. Think of it this way: When a family has two children, a father might say to one or both of them something like, "Son, don't do *that*. Honey, why are you doing *that*? I know you can do better than *that*!" His instruction will be personal, direct, and engaged. Add a few more kids to the mix, and his instruction becomes a little more formal, structured, and less focused because he has more children to watch.

When the family grows to include more than two children, the family management needs some additional structure to remain effective. The same is true with the church. The church grows to a size that requires more structure to give it the proper oversight and direction. It sounds simple, but this need can be shown in basic things, such as ensuring that events start on time and little details are not missed.

Growth makes mission, vision, and opportunity the driving factors. Relationships are still the glue that holds everything together, but the network of relationships is found in smaller departmental expressions where the organizational connections are formed. In the developmental stage, relational connection is the focus, and ministry is its by-product. At that stage, relationships attract people, who might say, "I know you. Why don't you come and be a part of our ministry? We have a really great thing going on here." However, at the structural formation stage, the vision, values, and mission become central to people's understanding of the church. They ask things like, "What is the mission of your church?" and "I have a heart for the homeless. What are you doing to minister to the needs of people?"

People minister to people. That fact does not change with any stage of development, but the size and scope of the ministry do change, along with the ministry's impact. Therefore, the church must implement a more formal process of leading people to make sure they engage with the church. Without question, people still come for connection, but they focus their attention on ministry impact as they consider their involvement.

In the structural formation stage, leadership and administration require more time, which leads to increased stress. It becomes increasingly difficult to maintain deep relationships because they are formed around ministry connections. Those connections may lead to friendships rather than friendships leading into ministry connections. Also, if the ministry connections change, then the friendships may become strained or lost.

As you recognize these dynamics at work in the relational interactions of ministry, you will know that the church is moving to another stage of development. When a child enters puberty, there are certain noticeable signs, such as a change in the tone of voice, increase in appetite, and a growing awareness of the opposite sex. Likewise, when a church is moving into a new stage, there are also telltale signs: difficulties in building relationships, departments building ministry silos, and disjointed and disconnected ministry perspectives. When those in leadership begin to say that they feel uninformed or complain about the loss of personal connections, you will know that you are moving from the *developmental* stage into the *structural formation* stage.

What once worked effectively for oversight and leadership simply out of friendship is no longer as effective. Frustration begins to increase for you and sometimes for the entire organization. At this point, people and programs that worked in the past become less fruitful, and turf building begins. Decision-making becomes slow and frustrating, and people do not feel empowered or connected. When these things begin to happen, if things do not change, people will disengage and ultimately leave. They will justify their disconnection or departure with statements such as "The leadership has changed" or "Things aren't the way they used to be. This place used to care about people but not anymore."

The Maturation Stage

The third stage of growth is the *maturation* stage. In this stage, *institutionalism* may become the focus, rather than the vision or relationships driving the work of ministry. By institutionalism, I mean the *things that we have created* now become the focus and the priority. We want to see them maintained, and maintenance overtakes growth. People become protective of their part of the ministry, their methods of ministry, and their pet ministry programs. They express resistance through nostalgia. They say things like "No, wait. Sister Mary's done that forever. We can't stop her from doing that!" Or they resist the necessary changes to programs with statements such as, "We've had this particular ministry since the beginning of the church."

When institutionalism sets in, we no longer embrace the things that are alive and powerful. Instead, we protect the past by valuing it over what God wants to do in the future. We must not let institutionalism fossilize the ministry; instead, we should lead the church back to its focus on God and people so that it can once again implement responsive and scalable ministry and accommodate current and future growth. We put systems in place to foster community. The church, regardless of its size, is a community; it can never be an institution. It is a living, breathing organism, and we must treat it that way. We must put systems in place that allow and foster the expression of community while maintaining a steadfast focus on hearing, believing, and obeying God.

In the maturation stage of the organization, we must identify, define, and embrace the governing and oversight roles that are necessary for the organization to function effectively. We must also implement the systems needed to protect and impart the organizational values, vision, and culture. By doing these things, we can release people into ministry. Recruiting, training, and empowering people for ministry allows the organization and its ministries to mature without becoming institutionalized.

Final Thoughts on Implementing Change

As we lead the church, we must openly acknowledge the governmental form we want to implement and teach the church the biblical rationale for it as part of the implementation process. Once we recognize our church's current stage of growth and formulate our plan with the end in mind, we can be confident that people will adjust and follow.

Do you want to build your church governance with a singular head and a plurality of leadership? If so, begin to develop the thinking processes necessary for your congregation to embrace that change. Be aware that the separation of roles and responsibilities is easier to understand and implement as your church moves out of the developmental stage. Regardless of your church's stage of growth, it should not keep you from beginning the process of change. Simply make sure that you begin with the end in mind. Healthy church government is one of the most essential factors for the strength, stability, and growth of your church.

No church can achieve its full impact, grow to its largest capacity, or develop the full scope of its God-given calling for ministry if it does not have an organizational structure and government that can support it. Healthy government and healthy structure create a framework for God's work to be expressed in ministry and for consistent growth to occur. I encourage you to be committed to these principles.

I am praying for you even now as I write these words. I am asking the Lord to work out His purposes in your life and to empower your ministry. I pray that God will help you as you evaluate and make changes under the direction of the Holy Spirit. I ask the Lord to lead you to a place where you can create a healthy government for your church so that God can work powerfully through your ministry and do miraculous things in your midst.

> Now to him who is able to do far more abundantly than all that we ask or think, according to the power at work within us, to him be glory in the church and in Christ Jesus throughout all generations, forever and ever. Amen (Ephesians 3:20–21 ESV).

Changing Your Style of Government

Key Thought

To be successful, a church must have a structure that establishes governance, provides operational authority and accountability, and aligns the responsibilities of all its members. Change is a part of a healthy atmosphere and necessary for growth; however, change may not come easily. It will take time, patience, and a tenacity rooted in obedient faith. You must develop a positive attitude toward the change among your church members and staff, and you must plan and strategize with the end in mind.

Summary

All churches go through stages of growth and maturity. These stages include:
- The Developmental Stage: Vision and values are instinctively defined as the core leadership emerges.
- The Structural Formation Stage: The management of growth and the formation of systems and structure to

facilitate the work of ministry emerge as the central issues.

- The Maturation Stage: Governing and oversight roles are identified, defined, and embraced, and systems are implemented to protect the organization's values, vision, and culture.

Group Opener

Turning a church in a new direction is a process that must be done with a positive attitude, grace, and care. As you begin to answer the questions below, ask the Holy Spirit to give your church a strategy for making positive change.

Group Questions

1. How can we begin to review the current condition of our church's structure from a governmental standpoint?
2. How can we begin to develop consensus for the changes that need to take place?
3. How can we help people and programs make the transition?
4. How do we begin to strategize with the end in mind?
5. At what stage is our church's current development?
6. How do we begin to implement, in a sensitive way, the things God is speaking to us?

Challenge

In the days and weeks ahead, explore on a deep level the areas where change must take place in your church. Don't get in a hurry but be intentional and press forward into what the Lord is saying to your church.

Prayer

Father, we ask You to guide our steps. We want to be a healthy church that is moving forward in the vision and purpose that You have designed for us. Our hands and hearts are open to what Your Holy Spirit is saying to us. In Jesus' name, Amen.